FROM THE ROOTS UP

A CLOSER LOOK AT COMPASSION
AND JUSTICE IN MISSIONS

JOANN BUTRIN

FOREWORD

John D. Rockefeller spent millions of dollars on a study to determine how to give money away without creating dependency. Most of this was done in Venezuela, but it encompassed many other countries where he was helping with various projects. I don't know what the results of that search were for him, but we do know through almost 100 years of missionary work now, that it is essential we get our missiology right before we do anything in the area of compassion ministries.

This book, *From the Roots Up: A Closer Look at Compassion and Justice in Missions*, written by our own Dr. JoAnn Butrin, has the answers to many of these questions. The book closely looks at the scriptural mandate to turn our eyes to the poor and to those who are treated unjustly. The Bible has so much to say about both of these subjects, and I'm glad that as a Fellowship we can address many of the issues of the world. Of course, our resources aren't enough to cover them all, but we can do our part, and I'm grateful that in so many ways we are now expressing the love of Jesus Christ to our needy world.

Dr. Butrin's book helps us know how to do this correctly. It is useless for us to throw money at every problem and think we're solving the world's needs. It has to be done correctly, with the principles outlined in Scripture that Dr. Butrin has so ably laid out for us.

I believe this book is vital for our day, and I trust it will be a guide for our future activity in this realm. We do need so much to respond to the needs of our world, but we must do it right so we don't create a worse world when it's all over.

L. John Bueno

Executive Director

Assemblies of God World Missions

A C K N O W L E D G M E N T S

I want to give many thanks to my friends, Carol Young and Rosellen Mientkiewicz, whose support and encouragement kept me going on this project. Thanks to Carol for all of the articles and ideas she sent my way. There were many early mornings, late nights, weekends, and airplane hours that comprised the reading, studying, and writing for this book. I often wanted to give up, but my friends and colleagues urged me on, telling me that one day it would come to an end.

I also want to thank my executive director, Dr. John Bueno, for his support and encouragement.

Thanks to Brandy Wilson for her work on the cover design, spending many hours to find the perfect "tree," and to Cindy Hudlin for her invaluable suggestions on content.

Thanks to Jami Pool, Paul Smith, Neil Ruda and Peggy Johnson-Knutti for their fine editorial work.

And lastly, thanks to my missionary colleagues and friends who work so diligently in compassion ministries, touching the hurting and bringing the Good News to those in need of His love and care.

CONTENTS

PREFACE

I have been in missions for what seems my whole life. I have lived and worked "among" the African people. I have learned two languages; I have breathed another culture for fourteen years. I have traveled to many other countries and cultures and have observed first-hand missions practice, and have seen every form and function of this practice that can be imagined. I have heard first-hand the hearts' cries of missionaries who have been touched by the needs that they see around them and have seen their sincere attempts to meet those needs.

As a new missionary, I didn't have a clue about "best practice" in missions, or social outreach or development. I didn't know anything about capacity building, local ownership, allowing solutions to come from the ground up—I was truly a neo-colonialist but didn't know it. I was fortunate to work with a very loving, forgiving group of people, and later learned about all of those things and did at least have a second chance. Not everyone is so blessed.

I have spoken with dozens of new, candidate missionaries, fresh with call and vision, dreaming of changing nations and winning thousands to Jesus. They are so full of compassion for the poor orphans, street kids, prostituted women, and the physically and spiritually impoverished of the world. I am so touched by their fervor and passion and so worried by their lack of training and knowledge. I wonder how they will go about meeting these issues that they have already perceived to be the most important needs that they should address.

I see young people in our churches today so full of passion and conviction that they can make a difference. And they truly can. Yet I wonder where they will receive the education and training so vital to understanding the issues of poverty and development and integrated mission. I want so much for their dreams and energy to stay alive and to be channeled into amazing productivity in ministry and missions, but see them forming nongovernment organizations (NGOs) and taking off to experience their "change-making" fresh out of school with little or no specific preparation for the task at hand.

I see our churches in the US, amazing in their spirit of generosity and willingness to help. I have been so impressed by their responsiveness when presented with needs both at home and abroad. Yet I also see that there are few avenues of missiological education available to the local church, especially when it comes to compassionate outreach, and each group tends to do what it deems best.

I've known and worked with a number of national churches too, who are, at times, caught in the middle. They have a vision for the work God is leading them to do, but feel a need to respond to donors' or missionaries' visions because they are the ones with the resources. Not wanting to offend, yet not really wanting what is being offered. Often, out of courtesy they will give a nod of consent to whatever the missionaries wish to do and continue on with what they feel is God's direction for their church and community. This is not always the case, of course, but unfortunately, not so uncommon.

Social justice is a phrase receiving much attention these days, as well it should. The tragedies of human trafficking, HIV/AIDS and the devastating effects of poverty especially on the lives of children and women are so alarming. Yet, as we so boldly set off to challenge these injustices, do we also contemplate that part of justice has to do with the dignity of the people who are unjustly treated? By disregarding the thoughts, ideas, and opinions of those we wish to serve, we may heap on them further indignation. Justice issues go far beyond the symptoms we can see and reach deep into the structures and systems of societies and cultures. Most of us from the outside are not adequately prepared to address these issues without really understanding what is going on. It takes times, study, prayer and relationships with those who know what is really happening.

I feel there is a need for us as Christians, as missionaries, as sending agencies, as receiving agencies and as the Church at large, to take another look at our response to the needs in other parts of the world and even in our own communities. Often referred to as compassion ministries, social justice, social concern, and humanitarian ministries, there is ever growing popularity for individuals, local churches, districts, missionaries, and sending agencies to be involved in this arena of ministry. Yet there is also a trend to feel that *any* response is an appropriate response because it is better than doing nothing in a world where the needs are so great. The Bible does, after all, compel us to "give to the poor" and "have pity on our brothers in need." I believe we need to examine those passages concerning justice carefully.

It is the hope of the author, that by the end of reading this book, there will be an understanding that unless the response is well thought out, done with and identified by the people who are affected by the issue and not for them, and done in a manner that will not create dependency, it may be better to do nothing at all. However, this book will also outline appropriate ways of responding that will be both effective, sustainable, and give outlet for the amazing generosity of spirit that God does want and implore His followers to demonstrate.

THOUGHTS FOR CONSIDERATION

Truth which is not clothed in life lacks real authenticity (Cheyne, 1996).

People do not only have souls that we register for heaven; they also have bodies that need to be taken care of. They have not only ears to hear what we have to say; they also have eyes to observe whether we truly live according to what we proclaim. There is no authentic mission without the motivation of love and the practice of compassion (Chester, 2002).

CHAPTER ONE

INTEGRATED MISSION: A HOLISTIC APPROACH

There was a cloud of dust as the old pickup truck pulled to a stop behind the house that I shared with missionary Peggy Johnson-Knutti in that remote jungle setting of the Ituri forest of Zaire, Africa. Four 55-gallon drums full of donated clothing had finally arrived from their very long journey from the United States. The dear ladies of Women's Ministries had collected shirts, slacks, and shoes, specifically for our lepers who resided in the leper colony nearby. Finally, after ships, trains, and trucks and months and months en route and hundreds of dollars in freight and customs charges, the long-awaited shipment had arrived at our back door.

The line formed and though taking pictures of leprous deformities was something my coworker and I just couldn't bring ourselves to do (despite pressure from donors), it would have made quite the newsletter story. Many were missing limbs, feet, hands, fingers, ears, eyelids, and parts of noses. Most had some sort of stick to aid their walking and many were in tattered clothing or rags. Yes, they did need some new clothes and there was a buzz of what I determined to be excitement as they each came forward to be handed a shirt and pair of pants that seemed appropriate to their size.

I was young, inexperienced and not what I would call overly tuned in, yet I knew that I sensed something amiss. There were nods of appreciation and expressions of it as well, but it was not in their eyes. In fact, quite the opposite. I thought I could almost detect anger. Later, as the group seemed reluctant to disburse, a spokesman was sent to inquire as to why there were no socks and no belts? I felt a little indignation at that point. All the money that had been spent to bring these nice clothes; that reeked of ungratefulness to me. Socks and belts, indeed! I really didn't get it. Yet in my heart, I knew there was something wrong with this picture—something very wrong with lining them up and giving them a handout, and it wasn't setting well with them either.

Wasn't this, after all, a tangible demonstration of our love for them? Wasn't this what the Bible was talking about when it said that we were to love in "word" and "deed"? We did do Bible studies with the lepers. We did preach in their church on the occasional Sunday. But this, this was the "deed" part. This was really showing something tangible, wasn't it?

I wonder why I didn't just ask them how they felt about it.

WORD AND DEED

There are so many passages in the Bible that instruct believers to care for the poor, to look after the orphans and widows, to follow the example of Jesus and to love in word and deed.

> "Dear children, let us not love with words or tongue but with actions and in truth" (I John 3:18, NIV).

> "For he stands beside the poor and hungry to save them from their enemies" (Psalm 109:31, *The Living Bible*).

> "He is the God who ... gives justice to the poor and oppressed, and food to the hungry. He frees the prisoners. ... He protects the immigrants, and cares for the orphans and widows" (Psalm 146:6, 7, 9, *The Living Bible*).

One cannot read the Bible and not see that the whole gospel that Jesus preached and modeled dealt with the physical, emotional, and spiritual needs of the people that he encountered both in community and individually.

Luke 4:14–21

[14–15] Jesus returned to Galilee powerful in the Spirit. News that he was back spread through the countryside. He taught in their meeting places to everyone's acclaim and pleasure.

[16–21] He came to Nazareth where he had been reared. As he always did on the Sabbath, he went to the meeting place.

When he stood up to read, he was handed the scroll of the prophet Isaiah. Unrolling the scroll, he found the place where it was written, God's Spirit is on me; he's chosen me to preach the Message of good news to the poor, sent me to announce pardon to prisoners and recovery of sight to the blind, to set the burdened and battered free, to announce, "This is God's year to act!" He rolled up the scroll, handed it back to the assistant, and sat down. Every eye in the place was on him, intent. Then he started in, "You've just heard Scripture make history. It came true just now in this place" (*The Message*).

In this passage, Jesus lays out for the believer, his theology of "whole gospel." He clearly starts with salvation and its availability for all who are willing to receiving it. It is a starting point, but not all there is to the "whole gospel."

Jesus made reference to the availability of physical healing. I cross-referenced back to Isaiah 61:1. It refers to the care of the broken-hearted. This signifies how Jesus pours a "soothing balm" on the emotionally hurting to bring peace and calm to those who weep and mourn. One can see how the "good news" includes compassion for the sick and the sorrowful, not just those in spiritual need. Scripture depicts consistently how Jesus ministers to the blind, lame, broken-hearted, destitute, marginalized, and downcast. He forgave their sins. He healed their body, soul, and spirit (Stearns, 2009).

In the same passage, Jesus goes on to speak of "proclaiming freedom for the prisoners" and "releasing the oppressed and to proclaim the year of the Lord's favor" (Luke 4:18–19, NIV). This is making reference to the Old Testament's Year of Jubilee when slaves were set free, debts forgiven, and land returned to its original owners. This was God's way of bringing balance to the economy and keeping the rich from getting too rich and His way of creating justice for the poor.

The Old Testament shows the evidence of God's concern for justice. Jesus' statement found in Luke makes clear that abundant life here and now includes salvation through faith in Christ, physical and emotional healing, healthy relationships, and justice for the poor (Stearns, 2009). In this perspective, the "whole gospel" is good news for the world and great news for the poor.

PENTECOSTAL WITNESS

"The Spirit is upon me," Jesus said. As Spirit-filled believers, we have the power and anointing of the Holy Spirit to be His witnesses and to follow the pattern of Jesus in *holistic* ministry. With the leading and guiding of the Holy Spirit, insight and greater human understanding can be gained, and supernatural healing and hope offered. Ministrations of compassion that come from Spirit-led motivations bring results that often touch heartfelt as well as temporal needs. That we, as Christ's followers, are to be concerned and actively involved with the needs of others seems to be beyond argument. The Pentecostal distinctive of Spirit-filled, Spirit-led believers should be that of ministry which goes forth with anointing, power, supernatural guidance, insight, wisdom, healing, and with the capacity to bring transformation of lives, communities, societies, and nations at every strata of life.

WESTERN VIEWS OF HUMANITY

Missionaries and ministers believe ministry needs to occur to the whole person. However, it does not seem to happen in this fashion. We tend not to integrate in our approach to ministry. It may partly result from how we have been acculturated. From the traditional western cultural influence, our cultural influence causes us to dichotomize or compartmentalize ministry in the way we compartmentalize our view of individuals.

In Western culture, we tend to compartmentalize a person into body, mind, and spirit. We go to a doctor or seek medical care for our body, we see a counselor or psychologist for our emotional/mind problems, and we go to the church or pastor when we have a spiritual problem. As we segment the person into parts, we often then take a dualistic or segmented approach to ministry, addressing the part to which we feel called to minister.

The person in theological education may feel "called to educate the mind." The church planter/ preacher/evangelist may feel called to minister to the "spirit or soul." The compassionate ministries or social concern person may be called to "care for the body."

Traditionally then, we have the so-called spiritual ministries which may consist of theological education, church planting, discipleship or evangelistic efforts. We then speak of compassionate or social ministries such as medical work, children's work, schools, feeding programs, care of orphans, economic development programs or disaster relief as a different category of ministry and somehow not on the spiritual ministry list.

NON-WESTERN VIEWS OF HUMANITY

Much of the non-Western world does not make the distinction that westerners do in their view of person. Body, mind, and spirit are seen as a whole. One of the parts is rarely addressed separately.

Persons in some cultures will often seek additional care, at a local or traditional healer, if their medical visit treats only the physical and leaves spiritual/emotional/social needs unaddressed. Persons will seek alternative care if the Church fails to address healing in a physical and social sense as well.

Western practitioners, working in non-Western settings, may find that in many cases churches, particularly those who have not been heavily influenced by western missionaries, have a DNA of social concern and have many activities that are addressing needs around them. They are birthed with a social conscience and see holistic ministry as an unquestionable part of the mission of the Church.

In their important survey of Pentecostals around the world, Miller and Yamamori (2007) discovered that many of the new Pentecostal churches that were being born in the last ten to fifteen years engaged in holistic ministry without needing to debate. Some interviewed said that it would be wrong to preach to people about the state of their soul when they are hungry, homeless or ill. These same individuals argue that simply meeting their physical needs would not provide long-term solutions to their problems (Miller & Yamamori).

EVANGELISM AND SOCIAL ACTION

If one truly grasps the message of "whole gospel," it doesn't seem necessary to use the word *priority* when speaking of evangelism and social outreach. It doesn't seem that Jesus was doing an either/or ministry but rather a both/and, at the same time. "Your sins are forgiven... Get up and walk" (Matthew 9:5, NIV). As Spirit-filled followers of the instruction of our Lord, we "have received power to be His witnesses to the uttermost parts of the world," and in our own "Jerusalem." The implication is clear. We are to go, to witness, and to make disciples. We are to proclaim. The Scriptures do not let us opt out of the proclamation, as some would like to say. Our doing good, or good works in and of themselves are not enough. We do not embrace the *social gospel* that allows for humanitarian good deeds to be a demonstration of the love of God, with nothing more needed.

Though many like to quote the popular words of Saint Francis of Assisi who said, "Preach the gospel at all times, whenever necessary use words," and though we understand the probable message that was intended, the fact is, people *do* need to hear a clear, adequate message of who Jesus is and what His death and resurrection means to their eternal life. We do need to use words; they are necessary if we are to transmit life-changing good news to the world.

The writer James described the heart of Jesus' mission when doing both/and of word and deed.

What good is it, my brothers, if a man claims to have faith but has no deeds? Can such faith save him? Suppose a brother or sister is without clothes and daily food. If one of you says to him, "Go, I wish you well; keep warm and well fed," but does nothing about his physical needs, what good is it? In the same way, faith by itself, if it is not accompanied by action, is dead (James 2:14–17, NIV).

Neither can we only proclaim and ignore others' individual needs. We should care for the poor, marginalized and broken-hearted, and seek justice for all. Lupton (2007) shares the following:

When we opt for rescuing souls over loving neighbors, compassionate acts can soon degenerate into evangelism techniques; pressing human needs depreciate in importance, and the spirit becomes the only thing worth caring about. Thus, the powerful leaven of unconditional, sacrificial love is diminished in society and the wounded are left lying beside the road. When we skip over the Great Commandment on the way to fulfilling the Great Commission, we do great harm to the authenticity of the faith (p. 16).

Proclamation loses its integrity, according to Cheyne (1996), when it is broadcast wholesale without dealing with persons individually in their real life situations. Truth which is not clothed in life lacks real authenticity (See 1 John 3:17).

Peter Kuzmic, author, professor, and missionary from Croatia, states that proclamation of the gospel alone is unbiblical and counterproductive. He concludes:

> It smacks of religious propaganda and senseless proselytizing. People do not only have souls that we register for heaven; they also have bodies that need to be taken care of. They have not only ears to hear what we have to say; they also have eyes to observe whether we truly live according to what we proclaim. There is no authentic mission without the motivation of love and the practice of compassion (Chester, 2002, p. 158).

INTEGRATED MISSION AND MINISTRY

What does integrated mission really mean? If one ministers holistically, what does that look like? Integrated mission is the proclamation and demonstration of the gospel. An advocacy group known as The Micah Declaration, that speaks for individuals who cannot speak for themselves, declares:

> It is not simply that evangelism and social involvement are to be done alongside each other. Rather, in integral mission our proclamation has social consequences as we call people to love and repentance in all areas of life. And our social involvement has evangelistic consequences as we bear witness to the transforming grace of Jesus Christ. If we ignore the world we betray the word of God which sends us out to serve the world. If we ignore the word of God we have nothing to bring to the world. Justice and justification by faith, worship and political action, the spiritual and the material, personal change and structural change belong

together. As in the life of Jesus, being, doing and saying are at the heart of our integral task (*Integral Mission*, 2001, p. 6).

Some are called to preach, others to teach and others are more aptly suited to care for the physical/emotional needs of others, but I believe the mandate is that we are all called to care for the whole person. Our ministries, our mission's work, our programs, regardless of our own particular gifting and talents, give room for the whole gospel to be carried out in one way or another.

This implies that the Bible school teacher, though focused on Biblical education, cannot ignore the physical and social needs of the students that he or she teaches. In relationship with the students, the teacher feels for the entirety of their lives and together they seek ways to find solutions and minister to their needs—not handouts, but workable solutions that assist the students to gain more independence while not being burdened down by insurmountable problems.

This also means that the compassion ministry worker would focus on the needs at hand, but minister to the entirety of the person, which would of course include ministry to spiritual needs in the person's life.

The lepers mentioned at the beginning of this chapter were recipients of a gift. Those who gave the gift in the US were well-intended. We missionaries who arranged for the gift were trying to do a good thing. We wanted to help and show that we cared but we probably, without meaning to, added another bruise to those who were already dealing with wounded and tattered self-esteem and dignity.

The primary intent of this book will be to examine that one way or another which, in the opinion of the author, is where so many well-intentioned ministries, ministers, and missionaries miss the mark.

THOUGHTS FOR CONSIDERATION

*Compassion is a virtue that takes seriously the reality of other
persons, their inner lives, their emotions, as well as their
external circumstances. It is an active disposition toward
fellowship and sharing,
toward supportive companionship in distress or in woe
(Nouwen, McNeil, & Morrison, 1983).*

*If poverty is viewed as the absence of things, then the solution
is to provide them. This often leads to the giver or outsider
becoming "Santa Claus" bringing all the good things: food,
education, roads, and even proclamation of the gospel, while
the poor are seen as passive recipients, incomplete human
beings who are somehow made complete because of what they
have received from their benefactors (Myers, 1999).*

CHAPTER TWO

FROM THE ROOTS UP: WHAT DO PEOPLE REALLY NEED AND WANT?

"Why didn't we get any socks or belts?" the leper spokesman asked. "We have these nice pants and shirts but no belts. How are we supposed to hold our pants up?" These seemed like ludicrous statements to me. Here we were out in an isolated jungle mission station, in Zaire, Africa (now Democratic Republic of Congo), many miles from anywhere, an eight-hour drive to the nearest town, nothing but forest all around, and this person had previously been wearing rags.

Now suddenly, there was tension and anger in the air because the dear ladies in the United States had not thought to include belts or socks, or more personally, the two missionary ladies in front of this man had not thought to *ask* for socks and belts. "How could we have been so thoughtless?" was the clear implication.

What was this man really saying? What was the underlying anger that I thought I heard? What was that steely look in his and the others' eyes that didn't reflect the gratitude that was verbally expressed? Was it similar to what the Creekside Community Church members reported when they delivered Christmas presents to the poor families in their community and noted that fathers often went out the back door, too ashamed to see strangers giving their children the gifts that they were unable to buy for their children (Corbett & Fikkert, 2009)?

Persons were acting out of the compassion of their hearts in both of the above examples, yet something was going awry between the giving and the receiving.

A Closer Look at Compassion

Compassion is an interesting word. Literally it means with passion, suffering with or feeling the distress of another. Just as courage takes its stand *by* others in challenging situations, so compassion takes its stand *with* others in their distress. Compassion is a virtue that takes seriously the reality of other persons, their inner lives, their emotions, as well as their external circumstances. It is an active disposition toward fellowship and sharing, toward supportive companionship in distress or in woe (Nouwen, McNeil, & Morrison, 1983).

Jesus felt and modeled compassion constantly in His ministry. The word *compassion* is used twelve times in the New Testament, and nine of those times refer to Jesus Himself. A widow lost her only son. The son was all that she had left since she had no husband. Jesus was moved with compassion and reached out to resurrect the boy (Luke 7:11).

Jesus felt compassion when he saw the crowds with all manner of sickness and disease. He reached out and healed them (Matthew 9:36). Jesus felt compassion when he saw the crowd hungry and fed them (Matthew 14:14).

Jesus felt compassion for the two blind men and touched their eyes to heal them (Matthew 20:34). The father of a demon-possessed son begged Jesus for healing. He felt compassion and cast out the demon (Mark 9:22). Jesus felt compassion when He saw the leper. He touched him and healed him (Mark 1:41). Nouwen describes how compassion elicits hard work:

- It is crying with those in pain

- It is tending the wounds of the poor and caring for their lives

- It is defending the weak and indignantly accusing those who violate their humanity

- It is joining the oppressed in their struggle for justice

- It is pleading for help with all possible means, from any person who has ears to hear and eyes to see

- In short, it is a willingness to lay down our lives for our friends. (Nouwen, McNeil, & Morrison, 1983, p. 141)

Furthermore, Nouwen stated, "Compassion asks us to go where it hurts, to enter into places of pain, to share in brokenness, fear, confusion and anguish" (Nouwen, McNeil, & Morrison, 1983, p. 141).

When carefully looking at the definitions and attributes of compassion, it is seen as something that is not done from one to another as much as something done together. It implies an entering in to another person's situation, gaining perspective of what that situation really is from that person's or group's point of view, and then proceeding together to figure out what the solution might be.

This is often not how compassionate acts of kindness are carried out because it is a very time-consuming, long-term way of being kind and most of us would rather be in a hurry. Our nature, our culture, and our system is geared toward quick fix, high visibility solutions that get people out of their misery as fast and as efficiently as possible, often leaving the very recipients of the solution out of the process.

WHAT DO PEOPLE REALLY NEED

Often as outsiders, we see need through our cultural filters. Not being part of the culture to which we are sent, we cannot at first completely understand the root causes for the needs that we see.

We see that children are hungry, abandoned, on the streets, seemingly orphaned, and homeless, and our hearts are immediately touched and filled with compassion for their plight. We see shanty towns and slums and hundreds upon hundreds of people living in poverty conditions, and we cannot sleep at night from the sights that we have seen. We walk through hospitals and see people dying from AIDS and TB and malaria, and know that there have to be answers to these issues. We travel to rural areas and see that people have no clean water or sanitation, and immediately think of wells that could be dug and latrines that could be constructed. We see school houses that are made of mud and falling down, and churches in ill-repair, and our mind goes to the construction teams that could so easily and quickly put up school and church buildings.

Coming from a world of *have* to a world of *have not*, from a world where most things can be fixed to worlds where it seems that the problems just keep getting bigger, can be pretty overwhelming.

Often our initial response is somewhat kneejerk when confronted with need, and we begin to try to solve some of the immediate problems that we see. To rescue. To be the provider. Though these are very understandable responses, they are usually not very successful ones and usually not very sustainable. Often these type of responses leave the responder worn out and soon without resources. It also usually does nothing to actually address the root problem causing the issue and doesn't increase the capacity of the people involved. It also, in many cases, may actually do more harm than good in that it lessens the dignity of those involved by making them recipients of charity rather than participants in solutions.

POVERTY

Before one's response to human need can be truly understood, it is necessary to determine how poverty is caused, how it is viewed and defined. There are many different lenses from which it can be viewed and varying levels of sophistication of definition.

Volumes have been written on the causes of poverty, but simply stated, sin has caused the breaking of relationships so that they do not work, causing oppression, dysfunction, disempowerment, greed and selfishness, and systemic injustice at all levels of society (Chambers, 1997, Friedman, 1992, Jayakaran, 1999, Meyer, 1999).

Some, according to Meyer (1999) in his classic text, *Walking with the Poor*, view poverty as "deficit" or a lack. Poor people lack food, shelter, and clean water. They lack roads, schools, adequate land on which to grow food, and because of all these missing things, this view encourages the provision of them with the assumption that once provided, the poor will no longer be poor. Lack of knowledge or skills may be added to the list of deficits, including a lack of knowledge of the good news of Jesus, so that proclamation of the gospel will be included in the meeting of these deficits of the poor.

The problem with the above mentality, Meyer (1999) points out, is if poverty is viewed as the absence of things, then the solution is to provide them. This, he asserts, often leads to the giver or outsider becoming "Santa Claus," bringing all the good things: food, education, roads, and even proclamation of the gospel. The poor, then, are seen as passive recipients, incomplete human beings who are somehow made complete because of what they have received from their benefactors. This, though done with good intention, has two negative consequences. First, it demeans and devalues them. Our view of them, which becomes their view of themselves, somehow comes to look like they are defective and inadequate because they could not do or provide these things for themselves. We, the benefactors, were somehow blessed by God, but they were not. This attitude increases their poverty of spirit and tempts us to play God in the lives of the poor (Meyers, 1999).

Secondly, we can begin to believe that we are somewhat God-like, and our benevolence becomes more about us than about the people we are serving. It feels so good to make someone's life better and make their lives complete, and we at some level may come to believe that we are their "saviors" instead of God. Ultimately this is not good for them but also not good for us (Meyers, 1999).

Corbett & Fikkert (2009) feel that low-income people see themselves as inferior to others, instead of being created in the image of God. As benevolence is bestowed on them, it heightens this sense of inferiority and can paralyze them into taking initiative and seizing opportunities to improve their situations, thereby locking them in to their poverty states.

FEEDING PROGRAMS

Let's say, in response to seeing hungry children, a decision is made to start a feeding program as part of a new missionary's ministry. Funds have been raised on itineration for "children's work," so this seems a legitimate use of the funds. Local help is hired, a small kitchen unit is set up near the area where the children seem to gather on the streets. The plan is to have a puppet show with a gospel presentation and then allow the children to line up for food after watching the puppet show. The first day about forty children showed up, but the second day, over a hundred and by the end of the week, the kitchen had to be shut down because there were so many kids that they could not be contained in a line. The bigger ones pushed the little ones away, fights broke out and the little kitchen building was knocked down. For days, kids kept coming around but didn't want to see the puppet show when they found out there wasn't any food.

Feeding programs unless done in a highly controlled environment, (like a school) with a well-thought out program, rarely work because there is usually no end to the line and no way to sustain the needed income to support such an ongoing endeavor.

More will be discussed on this topic in the section under assessment, but it is important to think in terms of the root causes of hunger. Different settings will bring different responses, but it is always a preliminary question. Are people really hungry? If yes, then why? What is the root cause of the hunger? How can those who are hungry be helped in a way that will eventually be sustainable? How can the people that are hungry be involved in the solution? Is the solution appropriate to the culture and context? Does it make any sense to bring in food from the outside if food can be grown or purchased in country? What do the local people think the solution should be? Should outsiders be involved in feeding children, or should the local church and community care for their own? Is it better to invest in the community and allow them to raise up enough to feed their own children rather than making them dependent on food from an outside entity? Is a feeding program a "feel good" program for an outside entity and a good fund raiser, or is it truly serving a purpose of meeting an actual hunger need? These are just a few of the preliminary questions that should be asked when considering the issues of hunger and feeding programs.

The national church and/or community with whom the missionary is sent to work would be the best resource to consult about hunger issues. Any decision to deal with this issue should be made together.

Lupton (2007) states it well when he says, "Doing for others what they can do for themselves is charity at its worst" (page 31). Lupton has worked for years in the inner city of Atlanta, Georgia, and has found that, unless the people themselves are a part of coming up with solutions for their own problems and then actively involved in solving them, the community may be "bettered" but the people aren't changed and real transformation personally and on a community level doesn't occur.

There is something, Lupton says, in one-way giving that erodes human dignity. This kind of compassion subtly communicates to the recipient, "You have nothing of value that I desire in return." One-way mercy ministry, as kindhearted as the giver may be and as well intentioned, is an unmistakable form of put-down.

Lupton (2007) talks about clothes closets and food pantries where clothing and food are given out free and says that, even though we know that reciprocity builds mutual respect while one-way giving brews contempt, we continue to run clothes closets and free-food pantries and give-away benevolence accounts, and wonder why people aren't more joyful.

Let's say a local church decides to open a food pantry as Lupton (2007) describes. Members are asked to donate canned goods, volunteers are asked to come and organize the pantry and to run it on the designated days that neighbors are allowed to come and get canned goods or food items. A sign is hung in the pantry which reads, "Only 5 items per family."

This outwardly seems like a nice gesture for the church to do. But looking more closely, what message does it actually send to those who come? It is one-way giving but with limitations (only 5 items). We are asking nothing in return, thereby fostering dependency and placing the takers of our benevolence in a recipient position, which at some level will probably engender resentment, though outward gratitude may be expressed.

It is the easy way to salve our conscience that we are being outward centered and touching our community. Doing *for* people is always easier than doing *with* them. As Lupton (2007) stated above, this is *bettering* people but not *developing* them. We haven't helped them move forward in their lives, just encouraged them to continue in their present state of problems. Granted, developing or "doing with" people takes much more of our time and investment in their lives.

For example, what if, instead of the food pantry, the neighbors were invited to a church dinner to discuss how the church could best be of assistance in their lives. What, for example, if the question was asked, "What has been working for you in this community? What are some of the things that help you the most?" And then, after some positive questions go into things like, "What are the main needs in your lives?" Perhaps hunger isn't even an issue for them. Did we even know if they needed the groceries that they came to collect? Perhaps a drop-in center for their kids, (because most of them worked), might have been a much bigger issue. If food was a problem, would a co-op to which they and the church could contribute be a much better solution? Would they be willing to work it and volunteer and become actively involved? If not, then that would say that hunger was not as big an issue as they are saying, and it was only an issue if someone else would do it for them.

In our compassionate responses, we sometimes would prefer to take the route of the least amount of involvement that would still let us "feel good" about the social outreach that we are doing, not considering whether we are having long term impact, sustainable results, and really "developing people's capacities to help themselves" in the process.

The best way to know what people need is to ask them. The best way to get an honest response is to know them. The best way to know them is to live among them and be in relationship with them. People will tell you what they think you want to hear, especially if they don't know you.

Are you hungry? Yes. Would you like us to feed you? Of course! There. We have had dialogue with the people and they want what we have—and so often that is how the worst of our practices come about.

People really do want to be respected. They want to retain their dignity. They want to be treated like anyone else would want to be treated. But the poor are not often used to being treated in those ways. They get used to having their dignity trampled upon and put up with it to get their needs met. Their trust levels are not high, so to win trust seems to be critical to beginning valid work with the poor. That can't be done without time and relationship building.

Short-term missions to the poor will rarely be of benefit unless done in close connection with those on the ground who have solid relationships with those who are being helped. Even then one has to be so careful to be sure that those who will be served are not made to feel like recipients whose dignity has been stripped away just to receive a service that may be only a band-aid for an immediate problem but will not have a lasting impact.

The term "rice Christian" came into play in the early years when the social gospel movement began to take hold. People in some parts of the world would be made to listen to a gospel message and then asked to pray the sinner's prayer. They would then receive a bowl or bag of rice. Word spread that all you had to do to receive the rice was agree to pray the prayer. Onlookers began to report that there were many who were recorded as conversions by the missionaries, who went away unchanged but happily fed. What we don't know, of course, is how many, having heard that message, truly did have divine encounters with Christ and whose lives were forever changed. It is simply an example of the care that needs to be taken as we set out to build relationships, meet needs, and share the wonderful Good News of our Savior to a hurting world.

WHAT HELPS?

How do we truly know what people want and need? Ask them. We really do need to enter into dialogue with people when we are outsiders to understand what they want and need. But it is not a street corner conversation. Before we begin talking about need, it is important to begin the conversation with what is positive. What is working for them? What is best about their lives? What are they happy about? What brings satisfaction? If we jump right into needs conversations then we immediately establish an imbalance—they are in deficit somehow. More will be said about eliciting assets in later chapters, but it is always good to begin relationship building with the "haves," not the "have-nots."

There are many ingredients that need to be present before a true understanding can occur and/or a true partnership effort can develop that can be mutually beneficial and have long-term impact.

1. *Establishing Trust*—Before either the givers or
recipients of help can know how or what to do together, it is
essential that they trust each other. Trust does not happen
without time together. Covey (2009) points out that low trust
slows everything, every decision, every communication. It
creates hidden agendas, interpersonal conflicts, defensive and
protective communication in every relationship. Having trust,
on the other hand, gives a sustaining quality of life to all
relationships, he feels, changing and affecting every effort in
which we are engaged. People begin to trust individuals, groups
and churches when they see:

- Consistency

- Integrity at every strata of interaction

- Honesty

- Follow-through

- Results

- True caring (which becomes evident over time as trust
  is established)

2. *Listening*—As the above characteristics are being
demonstrated, an important ingredient that speeds the process
of building trust is when people realize that they are valued by
those who want to help. One of the ways this can be shown is
when those in need understand that their voice matters. Rarely
is the input of those that are poor sought. So often
interventions are done to or for the poor, not with them. When

recipients of any intervention are actually involved in the decision-making process of their own solutions, it communicates to them that their opinion and therefore, they, matter. The only way that can occur is through *listening.* Cross-cultural listening is often difficult as filters do not always allow for true hearing to occur. Language barriers can also distort the message. But an honest effort to ask open-ended questions that have a true intent of seeking the opinions, involvement, and solutions from those who are in need truly communicates a message of value to the poor and helps to create an atmosphere of cooperation and trust. It is critically important if an effective, long-term impact to any problem is being sought.

3. *Assessment*—Because of the importance of finding out what people want and need, an entire chapter will be dedicated to the discussion of assets and needs assessment. But critically important to include in this chapter is the idea that somewhere along the way, together, there will be a formal or informal assessment of what is available and what is needed. It is a step that is often missed and can cause a lot of wasted time and money in the long run. Recently on a relief trip, this step was missed. A container of food that had to be prepared by cooking was sent to people who had lost their houses, their stoves, and their dishes. Needless to say, it didn't make those affected too happy when they stood in line a long time to receive something they couldn't use. A quick assessment done on the ground with the people involved in the crisis would have avoided that huge, expensive mistake.

4. *Participation in Solutions*—What prompts you to give more? The person sitting by the road with a sign that says,

"Hungry, please give," or the one that says, "Willing to work for food"? Most people would probably think that the person who is willing to work might be a little more worthy of their donation. In any case, most people truly want to be a part of solving their own problems. Research in refugee camps following disasters has shown that the sooner people can be involved in some type of work to try to put some order back into their existence, the sooner they begin to heal from the trauma of what has occurred. It seems to help give them back a sense of control when so much of their lives has suddenly gone out of control.

Persons who live in chronic need and poverty often feel like life is out of control all of the time. When others come and want to help but give them little opportunity for opinion, voice or participation in the solutions, much less to allow the solutions to come from them, their sense of being out of control can be heightened. Even though the help might be needed and appreciated at some level, as in the Christmas presents for the children mentioned earlier, there is still a sense of helplessness that is not addressed and even advanced by their lack of inclusion.

By giving voice, and then by participation and facilitating people to be a part of the design and implementation of their own solutions, ownership of the end result emerges. The greatest benefit, of course, is that people begin to take pride in what they accomplish for themselves. If children have Christmas presents, or more importantly, food to eat, parents can feel good about being the providers. Their self-esteem at having accomplished the role of a providing parent has heightened and they *own* what they have participated in. By doing everything for them, we rob them of that ownership and sense of accomplishment. What parent wouldn't rather present their child with a new coat then have someone else give the child a coat?

I remember when vaccines became available in the Democratic Republic of the Congo (DRC). Many children died each year from the complications of measles, so it was indeed good news that the government was providing free measles vaccine. Getting the vaccine to bush areas and keeping it cold, however, was no small challenge for us, the transporters of the vaccine. I recall a time when we got stuck in a mud hole for many hours, and our hearts sank as we knew that that batch of vaccine would be useless by the time we reached our destination. In any case, in the village where my co-worker and I resided, we decided to give the organization of the vaccination program over to the villagers. It was led by the pastor and women's group. We simply stated that we'd provide vaccines for the entire area if they could come up with a schedule, an incentive to get the women to come with the babies, and organize the whole thing, which they did wonderfully well. The next year, when very few babies were lost due to measles, it was they who felt good about saving their own kids. Not the white person—not the outsiders, but they themselves who had taken pride and ownership in the process and the results.

And back to the lepers. How could we have handled that scenario differently? What could have been happening that caused that seeming undercurrent of anger? I cannot recall at any time in my dealings with these wonderful people having a meeting with them where we just sat down and talked about what they really needed. Though we often went to their village and dressed their wounds and took bandages to them, we offered Bible studies and spoke in their little church and even dined with their pastor, we never really sat with them as a group and just said, "So, how are you doing?" and "What are the things that concern you most?" These are people missing limbs and noses and fingers and toes, but I have to wonder if some of their responses might have been something like, "We worry about our children and what will become of them," or "It's really hard for us to keep our houses built because, with our limited mobility, we can't cut the trees for the walls and the leaves for the roofs."

It grieves me to this day that we never had those conversations. I'm sure that at some level they did appreciate the clothes, but given the amount of money it took to get those clothes there, I think about all we could have accomplished together if we would have sat down and had a plan, their plan, to put that money to what would have benefited them the most. Maybe we could have invested the money in something that would have multiplied it so that they could have hired someone to cut trees for them, or started a small co-op and if any was left over we could have gotten used clothing brought in from the town down the road. But we never asked. We just assumed what they needed and then assumed their gratitude as well.

THOUGHTS FOR CONSIDERATION

*Compassion for those in need isn't an "add on" task to those
who are in Christ, or the Church as a Kingdom organism. It is
the essence of the Church of Jesus Christ. To be incarnational
is to be truly compassionate about the needs of others.*

*The Church is about caring for people, their spiritual, physical
and emotional needs, in all the world, in the name of Jesus
and by the power of the Holy Spirit—in other words, Missio
Dei, the mission of God.*

.

CHAPTER THREE

THE CHURCH TRANSFORMING THE COMMUNITY

Earthquakes, tsunamis, hurricanes, fires—natural disasters that dramatically and often tragically alter people's lives in a just a few moments of time. The church can rise up and be at its most generous during these times. As the media brings these tragedies to our viewing, no matter where we are in the world, our hearts are touched and the Church responds in offerings of money, donations of goods, and often in volunteerism of persons willing to go and assist with the crisis. From the poorest to the richest of churches around the world, there

seems to be a DNA of help to those in need during crisis …
usually … sort of … selectively … in most cases … but not
always.

My thoughts go back to the mid 1980s when the HIV/AIDS
crisis was beginning to be named and known. Its first
identification was that of a homosexual and hemophiliac
disease as those were the two populations in whom it was first
found. Later, of course, it was discovered in other groups as
well, but the label of homosexual disease seemed to have
particularly stuck in the minds of Evangelicals. As the crisis
began to pick up momentum in the USA and person after
person began to die from the illness, particularly gay men, the
church was strangely absent from the forefront of the crisis.

Most affected by the HIV/AIDS crisis is the continent of
Africa. Entire populations have been affected by the disease.
Often those between the ages of 15 to 34 are most affected,
thereby depriving the communities of their productive
members. In the early days of the HIV crisis in Africa, the
church there too was still highly absent as a main player in
those that were giving the issue the most attention. Stigma was
rampant, even in the church, and the hearts of the people were
not readily touched by the issue. The arms of the church were
not, in most cases, flung wide open to offer safe shelter and
help to those who were ill, suffering, desperate, and in most
cases headed to death, often without Christ.

The Church, which can be the greatest living organism of
faith, hope, love, comfort, and help, can sometimes be selective
and discriminatory in who and how it chooses to show the
beauty of Christ. That beauty that should be radiating from the

life of the Church as a steady beam to all within its reach and to the ends of the earth, is sometimes absent.

In some parts of the world, this has begun to change. Especially in Africa, the church in many parts of the continent has become a mighty force in addressing this crisis, in caring for its orphans and widows, and becoming activist in dealing with the forces of injustice that feed the epidemic and keep the needed aid from getting to the people who need it.

But sadly, in other places, particularly in the United States, the majority of the Church world has never seen this crisis as one with which to become involved.

One shining example of an Evangelical church in the United States which has led the way is that of Saddleback Church. Both in the US and abroad, the church has actively engaged in motivating its congregation to be engaged in practical helps for those with HIV/AIDS and has demonstrated its willingness to be a safe shelter to any and all who are dealing with HIV. They have provided tools and resources for other churches who want to be involved.

Sending donations or even volunteering for a disaster-related crisis is something we as a church do well. It makes us feel good, while helping someone else. Our motivation may well be good and come from a true compassionate response for those in need, but it's fairly easy. We can give what we have—clothes, money, even our time and energy to go—but then it's done. We don't have to deal with attitudes, grapple with different lifestyles, figure out theologies, and analyze our own fears of infection or our abhorrence of things we don't understand when it comes to responding to a natural disaster. It was just something that happened—an act of nature.

When it comes to AIDS, it a whole different story. It makes us have to deal with all the issues that were just listed. It makes us have to be reflective about ourselves and come face-to-face with issues that we'd often rather not think about as individuals or a church. Truly they are hard issues and don't have easy answers, but if the Church is the Church, as will be seen in these few pages, then there must be a place for everyone in the body of Christ. If the Church of Jesus Christ exists to touch the lost and hurting people of the world to bring glory to the Father, then it would seem that ministry and outreach to all people in all situations is what the Church should be about.

INDIVIDUAL AND COLLECTIVE RESPONSE TO NEED

The beautiful "Parable of the Good Samaritan" in Luke 10 is often quoted as Jesus' model of His expectation for the Christian's responsibility to those in need. It demonstrates a true commitment for a willingness to be interrupted and inconvenienced, to cross culture, and to provide immediate (relief) as well as a longer-term response to need. It is an excellent model for an individual's response when confronted with a need.

The Bible's instruction to the believer in Ephesians 2:10 makes it clear that there is no debate about the necessity of a response. "You are my workmanship," the passage states, "created to do good works." Each person, prompted by the

Holy Spirit and the compassion which wells up and motivates a good work, should respond to another generously and sacrificially, being willing, as was the Samaritan, to be interrupted, inconvenienced, and to continue that response over the long-term until it is no longer needed.

That means, then, being willing to do more than just drop a coin in the beggar's cup. If one is willing to be inconvenienced and continue the response over the longer term, then that would mean actually finding out why the beggar is begging, actually inquiring about the name of the beggar, where he or she lives, and maybe sitting down for a cup of coffee.

That certainly is inconvenient and takes a small act of kindness to a whole new level. Is that truly what Jesus was implying with this parable?

The Samaritan could have just dropped off the wounded victim and paid the innkeeper to make sure that he had all that he needed right away. But the passage says, he—that is the Samaritan—took care of him. We don't know how long he took care of him—a day, two days, a week—but the implication is that he did the care taking himself. Then he paid the innkeeper to continue the care until he got back, meaning he was going to come back that way and make sure he was okay and follow through with paying until he was well.

This was not a relief project not a one-time fix. This was a hands-on, interrupted schedule, caring response that was not convenient, but possibly life-saving and life-changing for this man. We don't know the impact that it had, but we could fill in that part of the story for surely that person left to die must have been in some way impacted by the compassionate care of this stranger.

The question which comes to mind when considering the parable of the Good Samaritan is, "What if there had been one hundred wounded persons along the road?" What could the Samaritan have done?

Thus far, we understand that God's Word mandates us to respond to other's needs. It has also been stated that without including the recipients of the response in the plan and/or with a kneejerk response, it is difficult to have an effective and sustainable outcome.

The parable of the Good Samaritan lays out a wonderful model for an individual response to human need, one that is not as easy to follow as it would seem at first glance, but one that gives a comprehensive, holistic response as a guide.

However, when the need goes beyond a few individuals, a collective response is usually called for, and that is when the body of Christ can be at its best—the Church, His Church—in response to the needs of the body which forms it and the community which surrounds it.

Jesus, during His time on earth, again set forth a model for his Church to follow in ministry:

a) sought and saved the lost in all the world,

b) discipled those who were saved,

c) compassionately demonstrated His love and care for those in need, and

d) gave glory to His Father God for all that was
   accomplished.

It is difficult, and really not necessary, for one person to
minister to the masses when the Church has been tasked with
just such ministry.

Compassion for those in need isn't an add-on task for those
who are in Christ or for the Church as a Kingdom organism. It
is the essence of the Church of Jesus Christ. To be incarnational
is to be truly compassionate about the needs of others. If one is
giving glory to the Father; i.e. in vertical relationship to God,
then the horizontal or outward extension of that relationship is
service to others, and that service is based in love and
motivated by compassion (1 John 3:17, James 2:14–17).

The Church, therefore, is about caring for people, their
spiritual, physical, and emotional needs, in all the world, in the
name of Jesus and by the power of the Holy Spirit—in other
words, *Missio Dei*, the mission of God. The local church, a
gifted body of believers, filled with the love and compassion of
Jesus, released together to touch the world, can bring healing,
harmony, and restoration to multitudes. It is the picture, I
believe, of what the church was intended to be: an organism of
salvation, reconciliation and restoration to the world. Truly it is
also a place of gathering together to worship and adore the
Lord, to build each other up, and to offer shelter and a place
where persons can find salvation, reconciliation, and
restoration.

When the Holy Spirit comes to a group of believers, a sense
of *koinonia*, which embodies unity and fellowship, reigns, and

with that unity of purpose and power and anointing, the body becomes able to sustain the reconciling message of Jesus' love to the sinner and hope to the downcast. It is that same power that gives wisdom in righting injustice, and power to come against principalities and powers that are not of the flesh and not always "seen or understood by human comprehension" (Ephesians 6).

WHY THE CHURCH?

1. *The Biblical Mandate is Clear*

    Most persons need to be sought before they seek, and sitting in the church waiting for the seekers doesn't quite seem to fit the scriptural pattern of outward focus. The missional sense of the Scriptures gives the sense of "release" or "thrust" of the believers into the world of unbelievers so that they might be found and discipled. As one examines the Scriptures, it seems that everything the Church is about has an outward focus—it's all about mission—going out, sending out, discipling those who are found and everything the Church does should be seen through the eyes of mission (Matthew 28:19, I Thessalonians 1:5–7, John 20:21, Mark 16:15,16). The world being the community in which the body of believers is placed (Jerusalem), closer communities (Judea and Samaria), and to the ends of the earth (world missions, Acts 1:8).

2. *The Church is Present*

    In almost every community, there is the presence of a church. Often there are multiple churches of different denominations. But the church is usually a part of the people and communities of which it is a part. That makes it a natural organism to become invested in the community around it. "If anyone has material possessions and sees his brother in need and has no pity on him, how can the love of God be in him?"(1 John 3:17, NIV). The church, hopefully is respected by the community in which it lives and breathes and as it interacts in vital fashion, it can become a part of the fabric and function of the community, participating in its needs, agonizing over its burdens, and bringing faith and hope through the Good News of Jesus.

The Church has become a sought-after delivery system by many organizations throughout the world for goods and services because of the breadth of its reach, because of its local context and because of its integrity. The US government's faith-based initiatives grew out of a sense that there was good reason to use this system to get directly to the people and be assured that those who were to actually get the service would receive it. The government organizations believed that the Church could be trusted to do what they said they would do and that they would be a trustworthy organism that people would look up to and follow.

3.   *The Church Understands the Context*

As opposed to outsiders, the local church on the field, in ministry to its own, understands the culture of those around it, usually can contextualize its message to be relevant to those it serves and, if it is in tune with its own community, is the agent who should be able to most effectively communicate the gospel.

When those from afar come to minister in an area not known to them, ministering in and through the local church, as long as it is a solid and relevant witness in its community, is far better than trying to be effective without it. It will greatly enhance the ability of the visiting entities to more quickly be understood and accepted. Conversely, if the visiting entity brings a needed and welcomed service or message to the community, the church's credibility and visibility in the community can be heightened as well.

In a restricted access country, I led a medical team on one occasion. There was one, small, struggling Assemblies of God church on the island. Never before had Muslims entered the church compound, but for medical care they came. The effort was seen as a gesture of kindness of that local church and the pastor reported that he and his church were seen with much greater respect after that endeavor. Where before he and his family were cursed and spit upon when he walked in the neighborhood, now he was greeted with kindness and respect.

I saw him recently, and he told me that his church had grown. Now he has a community center and a vocational training school, and things were going so much better. None of that work could have been accomplished without working hand-in-hand with the local church and its knowledge of the context.

4. The Church Has Influence

More than any other community system, the church has a strong and influential voice, at least to its congregants, and hopefully, to the wider community that it serves. It meets with its people regularly and frequently, and can become an informational voice because of those elements, which in areas where communications are limited, can be of major importance. For example, if vaccinations for children are going to be given at a certain place at a certain time, this information can be made known via the church for weeks in advance very effectively. AIDS prevention messages, and all sorts of public health and public service issues can be delivered via the informational systems of the church just due to the frequency of the gatherings. Church members, gifted with multiple talents, are often given to volunteerism. This provides multiple ways in which the church can participate in community activities, making it potentially a vital organism in the community that could greatly influence and impact the life of the community.

As the walls between church and community become transparent and the love of Jesus is shown and shared, lives are committed to Jesus, and the community is transformed by the power of Christ.

THE INDIGENOUS CHURCH

Much is spoken and written about the indigenous principles in missions, and some missions organizations ascribe to the indigenous principles as their modus operandi in their overall mission's strategy. In other words, the goal of their church planting endeavors is to ultimately have churches that are self-supporting, self-governing, and self-propagating (Allen, 1962, Hodges, 1953). Many have also added self-sending as matured, indigenized churches around the world and are now sending out their own missionaries to other parts of the world.

The word "indigenous" in its 21st century meaning, may, however, turn this concept into a negative if not carefully defined. In its broad meaning, indigenous can and does refer to an ethnic group or any group confined to a geographic location. When referred to long ago by missions organizations, it was meant to distinguish between those who were "sent," i.e. the missionaries, and those who "received" them, i.e. the national people or those who lived on the foreign soil to which the missionary was sent. The point was to pull away from the paternalistic, dependency-building, "great white mother and father" approach that had been done in early mission years, and rather help to establish works that would be independent and able to stand without the aid and influence of the missionaries and outside financial assistance. Thus *indigenous* was referring to "locally owned and operated by local people."

In a recent presentation, Dr. Ivan Satyavrata (2009), an Indian scholar and pastor, commented on the three-self notion—self-supporting, self-governing, and self-propagating—as a Western concept that would not be the norm for cultures and societies that were more community-oriented and would not relate well to a self-concept. He also proposed that autonomy and self-sufficiency might mitigate Jesus' calling to servanthood and self-denial.

Also, in today's understanding of the word, this definition, if taken literally, the establishment of an indigenous church could be interpreted to mean *one that is created to include only a certain ethnic group and/or to exclude other minorities or races.* That is not the intent of what is meant by the term in this book or by missions agencies.

It is perhaps the time to search for a more appropriate term, but for the sake of discussion, one will continue with the term indigenous to mean, *a strong, healthy independent work, which has its roots in the local culture, and is able to sustain itself and replicate itself if there is a need and desire to do so.*

In observing missions work in many parts of the world, it appears that the indigenous church planting movement has been interpreted in many different ways and has taken many different forms. One can observe excellent models where basic principles have been taught, perhaps in Bible schools, with at some point some foreign influence. Local nationals have caught the vision and established excellent, strong, healthy churches that are growing, replicating, and sending.

In other places, there are examples of strong foreign influence with pastors being paid by outsiders, churches being constructed by outsiders, Bible schools being subsidized completely or partially by foreign dollars, and in some cases, churches with pastors from the sending country. One can debate all of these practices, but from a self-supporting standpoint, the one that would stand out as least healthy would seem to be having a pastor being supporting by an outside entity, meaning the church would not be taking responsibility for its own pastor. Those points are listed simply to point out the diversity of practice (all these have been observed in one organization) in the following of the indigenous principles.

COMPASSION AND THE INDIGENOUS PRINCIPLES

As pointed out above, there is a great deal of diversity of interpretation in what the indigenous church principles really mean when it comes to missions practice. When it comes to social outreach or compassion ministries in missions, it seems the indigenous principles are often completely abandoned.

As stated earlier, the church is by far the richest resource of the community. It has the greatest potential of being the greatest beam of light and hope to its own people. It would seem to be one of the greatest reasons for its creation, to seek out those who are hurting, who are needy, who are afraid and who need shelter, and bring them to safety.

Yet, so often compassionate outreach, even that which is started by missionaries, is not done in and through the local church.

Here is a scenario often seen and heard from missionaries. "Well, the local church does not have a vision for the hurting community around them. God has given me a heart for the children of that community. Therefore I must reach out to the children. I wish the church wanted to do it but they don't, so I am doing it without them."

My question to these individuals usually is, "So if you become ill next week and need to leave, what happens to your program?" Another question, "Did you spend time trying to build relationships in the local church, with the local pastor and his wife? Did you try to share your vision for the children within the local church and build excitement and inspire those to come alongside and allow this to build from within the church rather than from within you?"

Sometimes, the problem is simply that it takes a lot more time to do it "from the roots up," to let solutions to the issues of the local communities to come from within rather than from the outside.

When it comes to missions, missionaries come with a "Let's get going attitude." They also come with funds. And the relationship building, vision casting, and waiting is really hard for most from Western cultures that tend to be more results-oriented and want to get things done quickly. Thus the idea of "indigenous" when it comes to meeting community needs or establishing compassion ministries through the local church often gets put aside because, after all, people are suffering.

There is no intent in this book to put down the foreign missionary as truly many good things have been accomplished. But the "savior" mentality is still with us when it comes to social concern. We have not, I believe, truly come to acknowledge that we can help best by helping people to help themselves. We still want to *do for*, instead of *do with*, or just do it ourselves.

If as missionaries, sending agencies, churches from the outside, and churches in communities, we can see and understand the amazing strength and ability of the local church to impact its own community and somehow learn to work with, in, and through the local church in all that we do, I believe that together we can truly have the greatest impact for the Kingdom of God and see the greatest harvest of lives for Christ.

Recently I took part in a medical relief effort for a flooding disaster that took place in the Philippines. It was a beautiful example of some of the principles listed above. Though there were American medical professionals on the team, the team was lead and organized by Filipino medical professionals, who were equal in number to the Americans. Funds were donated by the American group, but given over to the Filipino group to buy the medicines they felt appropriate. The national church leaders organized the sites of the team visits, and every day the relief clinics were set up in a local church that was near to the flooded areas. Food and clothing were distributed as well as medical care but all in the name of the church. It was not an American relief effort—it was a local church reaching out to its community and it just happened to have some American friends who came to help.

What Helps?

A local church or body of believers may not always have the same vision as a missionary or outside group for a specific need. The tendency is often to just get their blessing and go ahead without them. I would like to suggest that instead of this, which will ultimately result in a missionary-driven and missionary-dependent project or outreach, the missionary should step back and begin building relationships within the local church. Get to know the pastoral staff and their spouses. Get to know the people in the congregation. Find out what they are passionate about and what their resources are. Do the asset and needs assessment, outlined in later chapters, and just spend time with the local church and people of the community.

There may then be opportunities to teach classes and preach sermons on compassion and helping others, which might stir up burdens that were not presently there. Or the missionary may also find that what they were passionate about isn't really what he perceives is needed by the community. In the process the missionary may realize that what the church IS passionate about may be a greater way to invest time and resources.

Relationship building within the local body will allow for mutual sharing of burdens, dreams and visions. Ultimately, it will probably result in some type of friendships that will allow for working together on an outreach that will bless whomever it touches.

It does take time, however, to build those relationships, work through assessments, share each others' dreams, and become friends.

Friends want to help each other.

THOUGHTS FOR CONSIDERATION

*According to the biblical view of human life, transformation is
the change from a condition of human existence contrary to
God's purpose to one in which people are able to enjoy fullness
of life in harmony with God. This transformation can only
take place through the obedience of individuals and
communities to the Gospel of Jesus Christ, whose power
changes the lives of men and women by releasing them from
the guilt, power, and consequences of sin, enabling them to
respond with love toward God and toward others and making
them "new creatures in Christ" (Wheaton Consultation,
1983).*

CHAPTER FOUR

RELIEF & DEVELOPMENT FROM THE CHRISTIAN PERSPECTIVE

The scene will never leave my mind. The little six-seat Mission Aviation Fellowship plane circled over the smoldering volcano, then made its descent into the border town of Goma, Zaire (DRC), the cauldron of death. During those surreal days of July 1994, the shocking reality of the atrocities of the Rwandan genocide had not fully hit home to those of us who were arriving on the scene. Over eight hundred thousand people had been slaughtered in Rwanda in one of the worst genocides of our history. Over one million refugees fled into

Goma, Zaire, in fear for their lives. Then, tragedy struck once again. The cholera virus infiltrated the river from which they drank and one after another—hundreds a day—succumbed to diarrhea, dehydration, and death.

The stench of death hit full force as we left the airport and found transport into town. Tears involuntarily rolled down our cheeks as we saw body after body lying along the streets, in the fields, by the curbs, abandoned, alone, unattended or in a pile. It was so un-African.

As a health professional, I had seen a lot of death, but never in massive numbers. I'd seen a lot of tragedy and sorrow and tried to save lives before, but never had I or the others on my team experienced this massive suffering of humanity or this much death at one time. Never had we been faced with deciding who was to receive the limited IV solutions that were available. Who would actually get the drinking water that was finally delivered? Who in fact would live or die?

A child was crawling around among the dead bodies but no one knew where she belonged. No one was claiming her. Each day a truck would go through and pick up babies and children that were sitting by dead bodies and take them to a tent for unclaimed children.

I learned a great deal about relief and about myself in those days. The magnitude of the tragedy almost overwhelmed me. I experienced guilt when I had a bed to lie in at night. I struggled with guilt that I had food to eat when thousands of others practically outside my door had nothing. Additionally, I suffered guilt when I wanted to wash my hair and water was a scarce commodity. Yet, I still slept, ate, and washed because I had the resources. I came from the land of "have." That made all the difference. A massive relief effort to a little over a million people sustained primarily by media hype and huge planeloads of relief supplies began to dwindle as the media interest waned.

DEFINING RELIEF

Relief is what is called for when, due to circumstances beyond the control of the people affected, normal ways of coping with everyday living are taken away. Relief usually always involves a crisis situation and often requires the intervention of others until equilibrium can be reestablished.

Relief is and should be short-term in nature. It is usually controlled by outsiders; it rarely involves those affected as participants, but rather sees them as recipients. And if carried on very long it has great potential for very quickly developing a dependency by those receiving assistance. Though people may seem initially grateful for relief, being cared for by someone else for basic needs, over time, can make people feel a loss of dignity, and self-respect. It can destroy motivation for self-help.

Relief is critically important when natural disaster strikes, when wars or some sort of calamity comes for which there was no possibility to prepare, or if even the best preparations were not enough to endure through the enormity of the crisis.

Effective relief can often incorporate elements of rehabilitation and development from the start. This will help to eliminate the possibilities of dependency development.

People are often in a state of shock from whatever calamity has come to them and may not be able to think or act in a coherent fashion immediately. There is often such a feeling of helplessness and a sense of being out of control that it has been found to be therapeutic, especially for men, to be given tasks to do to help with the relief effort itself. So rather than being passive participants of relief, those affected can be engaged in the planning of food distributions, and can actually assist with distributions, organizing shelters, etc. The more people can participate in their own recovery, the more rapidly they are likely to recover (Relief Web, 2003, p. 4).

The sooner the relief situation can be turned toward development and people become involved in rebuilding their lives and doing meaningful work, the more likely they will be to recover. Attention to issues of grief, loss, and stress are very important. If those issues are not dealt with soon after the incident happens, they can stand in the way of motivation to do work and a desire to return to normal living and post-traumatic stress may occur later and continue throughout life.

UNHEALTHY RELIEF RESPONSES

One day there was a big storm. The monkey ran up in a tree for shelter. He looked below him and there was a stream. He saw a fish swimming among the rocks. The monkey said to himself, "There is a fish struggling in the water! He needs me to help him!" So he swung down from the tree branch and pulled the fish out of the water, and set the fish on the dry ground away from the stream. The fish was flopping around on the ground. "Look how happy the fish is!" the monkey said. Then the fish stopped flopping and became still and calm. The monkey said, "The fish is comfortable and relaxed now. Maybe he is sleeping. I feel so good that I helped this fish. Maybe I should go look for other fish I can help, too!" The monkey went away, very proud of himself for saving the fish (An Eastern parable).

Though the above scenario may seem somewhat extreme and humorous, it does serve as a segue into some thoughts on ways in which those with hearts to help and serve can do so in a manner which will have maximum benefit. It also points out how our best intended efforts may at times not be the best for those we wish to help.

The same good intentions that moves the new or short-term missionary to respond to the needs around them in ways that may not be the most appropriate, as mentioned in Chapter 2, may also motivate well-intended outsiders to respond inappropriately when disaster strikes another part of the country or the world, and relief is called for. Some of these less appropriate responses are described below:

GOING TO THE SCENE OF THE DISASTER

The first response of those who hear of a major disaster is often that of wanting to go to the scene of the disaster. This is often one of the most inappropriate responses. Most often major disasters are dealt with by "first responders," i.e., those who are nearby and who can get to those in need as soon as possible or usually within the first 24 to 48 hours of a disaster. That is often the most critical time when persons need rescue, shelter and food, which is often able to be delivered by those that are nearby. It is true that backup supplies and assistance will be needed as time goes on, but usually that will be delivered and distributed by agencies that are registered or equipped to do so. Extra people who arrive on the scene, unless specifically requested by governments or aid agencies, usually have to look for something to do, often get in the way of relief efforts, take up housing and food that is needed by authentic relief personnel, and spend funds that could be more adequately used to deliver appropriate aid.

Usually those who go are not adequately trained in disaster response and don't know appropriate ways of responding. Though wanting to help, much of their time is spent trying to figure out how to help, who they can work with, how to access the system of helping. It often turns out to be a disappointing time for the people who go and a burden for those who are trying to find ways for the "helpers to help."

SENDING MEDICAL TEAMS

Depending on the type of disaster, medical assistance may be requested, but most often and in most countries, medical personnel from the affected country who speak the language of the country will be the most qualified to meet the medical needs of the victims. In many disasters, initial assessments show that medical needs are not the most pressing of the needs, but rather shelter and food are more urgently needed. Often, however, when people hear of disaster and know that there are some injuries, the immediate response is to gather a medical team and some medicines and try to get both into the affected area. Some medical teams have been disappointed to find that they have not been allowed to enter, or their medicines have been confiscated. Others were not permitted to work as they had not gone through the proper procedures that would give them permission to practice in the country to which they traveled. One sometimes erroneously assumes that in the time of disaster, none of the usual rules apply, which is often not true.

CHRISTIAN WITNESS DURING RELIEF

At times, it is appropriate to send Christian relief workers to a non-Christian situation to demonstrate God's grace. As a rule, those teams need to be carefully chosen, culturally sensitive, and experienced individuals who know how to be exceedingly sensitive to the Holy Spirit and the culture and people with whom they are working. There have been powerful examples of the Lord using His people to be His hand extended at the time of disasters.

Usually, those at the scene have been Christian team members and/or missionaries with years of experience in dealing with disasters and peoples of various religious persuasions. The best scenarios are when the team can be coupled with local church members and Christians that can help them understand the culture and context and how to most effectively share the Good News with those they serve.

Donating Goods

Another well-intended response of those moved by the plight of others is that of giving of goods to send to the affected population. This may be a very appropriate response if the giving is done in direct response to what is being requested by the country or people affected by the disaster. Most often, however, what is needed, other than shelter, can be purchased in-country, and money rather than goods is more often what is requested. Most have heard stories of the wrong types of clothing that have arrived in containers, like heavy winter coats going to tropical climates, or party dresses or high heeled shoes, or food was sent that the receiving population would never eat. These are all well-intended but a waste of time, energy, and money. Likewise funds were no doubt spent on the other end to get rid of the things that could not be used.

Usually large missions agencies or government organizations have a pulse on what is needed in these types of disaster. But often because of not being willing to inquire or cooperate with those who know the need, individuals or churches do their own thing and end up not being highly effective.

Disaster Preparedness in High Risk Areas

Some parts of the world are known to be high risk areas for natural disasters and are prone to more frequent disasters than others. In these areas particularly, but in any area that would wish to be prepared, there are entities that offer disaster preparedness training for local churches and communities (Salvato, 2005). This type of training helps key pastors and community leaders to be aware of warning signals of impending disasters, helps them to have a disaster plan ready for implementation, helps them to stockpile supplies and food for ready access when disaster strikes, and helps them to know simple rescue techniques and simple first aid.

There have been several areas in which people have had this training and then had a disaster strike. They have given testimonials to the ways in which the training was immensely helpful in reducing death and injury and helping them to recover more quickly and efficiently.

It is unfortunate when developmentalists want to put down or lessen the role of relief on the world scene. In its place and when *done appropriately*, relief has a vital and important function. It is a wonderful outlet for the generosity of the human spirit, a tangible way for the body of Christ to respond to brothers and sisters in need.

FROM RELIEF TO DEVELOPMENT

As stated earlier, whenever possible, a relief effort should be turned towards helping people help themselves as soon as possible. That may be as soon as the relief effort begins in some cases, by involving the affected persons in the process of organizing and helping in their own recovery. At times, however, the disaster may be too large and too overwhelming, and the focus of the effort may be on survival and getting people to safety. Studies have shown, however, it is most beneficial to move relief into a rehabilitation and development mode within a matter of days of the actual event whenever possible (Relief Web, 2003, p. 4).

Development means a dynamic process that empowers people to identify root causes of problems and solve them permanently using local resources, and involves long-term strategic planning. Development activities should be done *with,* not *for,* the participants. It should thus be concerned with means that are the simplest, most cost-effective and replicable. Even children can and should participate in what affects their lives.

Transformational Development: Developing People

What this book wishes to address is development, as it relates to missions and missions endeavors, and to look at some comparisons between the indigenous church principles referred to in Chapter 3 and basic development principles in missions.

Before doing so, it is necessary to define terminology for the purpose of this book. First it is important to note that the word *development,* as used in this book, differs from the secular term, which can be more about program and less about people. *Development* from a missions point of view, and as used in this text, is about people. It's about transformation of the whole person, physically, emotionally, socially, and spiritually.

According to the biblical view of human life, transformation is the change from a condition of human existence contrary to God's purpose to one in which people are able to enjoy fullness of life in harmony with God (John 10:10; Colossians 3:8–15; Ephesians 4:13). This transformation can only take place through the obedience of individuals and communities to the Gospel of Jesus Christ, whose power changes the lives of men and women by releasing them from the guilt, power, and consequences of sin, enabling them to respond with love toward God and toward others (Romans 5:5), and making them "new creatures in Christ" (2 Corinthians 5:17) (Wheaton Consultation, 1983).

All references to development for the remainder of this text will be considered that of transformational development unless otherwise noted.

Transformational development will always have a goal of personal and community transformation from spiritual darkness into the knowledge of Jesus Christ and His liberating power. It will be concerned with allowing for the ability and capacity of individuals and communities to plan for and participate in the solutions to their own problems. In transformational development, solutions to problems arise from the grassroots and whenever possible, local resources are utilized rather than outside resources. Whatever process and programs are implemented, the ownership and involvement must be from those affected by the issue, not from the outside. If ownership of the process doesn't occur, the likelihood of ongoing sustainability is diminished. Participatory asset and needs assessment is part of the developmental process (see chapter 5 for more details). Sustainability, or the ability of any process or program to continue by the persons benefiting from it, is a hallmark of transformational development. Dependency on outside persons or funding is not a long-term expectation of development.

In transformational development, partnerships, though not excluded from the development process, are those which are equally entered into and have some negotiable way of seeing that the parties involved can have mutually satisfactory outcomes. Like the indigenous church principles, persons, communities or programs will become transformed and self-supporting, self-governing, and self-sustaining, and able to replicate, model, train, or send others to model what they have accomplished through their efforts.

From the onset of a development process, an evaluation process will be built into whatever is being undertaken, from the smallest task to a large church or community endeavor. This will enable those involved to measure the effectiveness of what is being done, establish timelines, and stay on track with the original ideas of the group.

Whenever possible, transformational development will happen in and through the local church if there is one available. In restricted access areas, a goal may be, as part of the process of transformational development, to plant a local church. But when available, the local church, for all the reasons listed in the previous chapter, is an excellent window into the community and a way in which Jesus can most beautifully shine light into the homes and hearts of those it serves.

Examples of Transformational Development in Missions

ONE—Instead of a feeding program, after several meetings and discussions, the local church committee, the missionary and community leaders might undertake a community assessment to figure out if and why children are hungry. Questions such as whether it is lack of food, improper food, agricultural techniques, lack of money at home, unemployment, alcoholism, etc., must be considered.

Based on the asset and needs assessment (see Chapter 7 on Assessment), a plan of action may be put in place that would address the root cause of hunger rather than just trying to feed the children. The solution may be to improve the source of food, or money, or start a business or a special garden or ... on and on the solutions could go. The goal is that the solutions would arise from the people affected, not the missionary, and the funds would be generated from within, though mission funds could be used as startup funds for whatever is proposed. This is a great way to invest missions dollars.

TWO—Children are sick and some are dying with diarrhea in a certain remote community due to unclean water. A missionary who resides in town but comes to visit is asked to help. The missionary could just ask the "clean water non-government organization" (NGO) to come and dig a well and provide clean water for the village. That would help, but a whole lot more could be done that would perhaps be of more help.

To provide immediate relief, the missionary knows of a sand filtering system that can brought in to provide immediate relief so the children can get clean water right away and stop being sick, and certainly stop the deaths. A couple of people of the village are chosen to be trained in its use. Missions dollars are used as a temporary solution to an immediate problem.

The missionary talks to the church and community leaders about the Community Health Evangelism program (CHE). This is a program that will train community individuals in sanitation principles and clean water. It will teach them how to clean up the entire village and get all the members motivated to take care of their own health issues. (Community Health Evangelism has a complete curriculum available through Life Wind. Training is also available through HealthCare Ministries. See <www.lifewind.org> and <www.healthcareministries.org> for more information.)

The leaders agree to choose several individuals to attend, and the pastor and community leaders decide to attend, as well. The CHE training takes a week and those who attend come back really excited about sharing this information with the village and getting things in shape. Eventually they will want to invite a group in to help them put in a new well for their village, but they want to participate so that the whole village will feel that it is their well and they will take care of it. They also want it to have a pump that they can maintain and fix if it breaks down. They feel that their latrines need to be fixed and moved before the well is put in so contamination doesn't occur.

Because they learned how to incorporate spiritual messages into their health teaching, they are seeing many new converts during the course of their family-to-family health instructions and group meetings.

The easy, fast way to solve the problem would have been to have some outsider come in and dig a well, but the long-term solution was what was done in this case study and the results of this will go on and on.

THREE—A certain community had lost many parents to AIDS and more and more children were being orphaned. Families, who would normally take the children in, were overwhelmed with trying to feed, educate, and care for their own children, and couldn't see their way to take in more of the orphaned children.

The missionary in this area had a team visit from the USA and one of the team members, noting this issue, upon returning home wanted to raise money to build an orphanage for this particular location. Getting a building team together to do it, as well as the funds for the building wasn't going to be a problem, the missionary was told.

The missionary did some research, though and realized, that to keep the orphanage running with a hundred children, provide staffing, food, utilities, health care, education, and all that would be needed, would require an enormous amount of money. He also read that institutionalizing children is not in their best interest, would rob them of knowing what a family is like, would strip them of knowing about their own culture, and would expose them to many communicable diseases. It would also not equip them for coping with the world once they left, would leave them with no family to go home to once they were out of the orphanage, and would leave them vulnerable to being abused or exploited by care takers or older children in the orphanage.

He went and talked with the local church leaders and asked them if they were prepared to take on such an institution. Although they weren't opposed to it, they were honest in saying that there was no way that they could financially support it.

Consequently, the church leaders and the missionaries started having some dialogue sessions about the orphaned children and invited a few of the more friendly community leaders. They knew the problem was growing and that the church needed to respond in some way, but they weren't sure what to do. They heard that there were some foster home models that another denomination was using and also some small church-based group home models, so they planned some field trips and went to investigate. It seemed that both models were based on starting some small businesses or micro-enterprises that would help boost the income of families to be able to take on extra children.

The missionary and the church leaders felt that these models would serve the children much better. They wrote up a proposal to send back to the church in the US asking if they'd be willing to invest the funds that they wanted to spend on the orphanage in helping them get a program like this off the ground. Unfortunately the church was not interested in this, but they did manage to find another organization who was and who had experience in this type of model. This organization helped them write a business plan. Their proposal was funded and they helped them set up a small for-profit organization that was run by a church-based committee to oversee the running of the fostering program. The missionary raised funds to invest in it as well, and a small shoe-repair business was formed. The assessment showed that to be what was needed, and the asset assessment showed the talents available to generate the funds to keep the foster program going. Families were screened and could apply for financial assistance to take in an orphaned child. Since it was church-based, the church could legally choose Christian families for the children.

These are just a few of many, many examples of ways in which development principles can be applied to missions activities that can produce Kingdom results.

COMMUNITY DEVELOPMENT

Community development is a term which incorporates much of what has been said earlier in the chapter. It is about the members themselves discovering what the assets and needs of their own community are and coming up with ideas on how change might take place. When the church and Christians are involved, it becomes transformational community development because it is concerned about the spiritual transformation of the individuals which comprise the community.

A church that cares for the community of which it is a part can undertake community transformation as a viable outreach. As stated in the previous chapter, the mission of the church is restoration and reconciliation of those within its reach. According to Ron Bueno (2009), Director of Enlace, a community development organization of El Salvador, "The church should serve its neighbors to create long lasting change in the relationships, institutions and overall conditions of their communities, especially focusing on those in greatest need" (Mark 12:31–33; Luke 10:27; Matthew 22:39; Romans 13:9; Galatians 5:14; James 2:8).

It is, however, according to Bueno (2009) who has worked with church/community development for many years, a slow, arduous, and evolving process. It first becomes evident by glimpses of transformation in people's hearts, values, and attitudes toward God and to each other. After many years, transformational community development encourages and produces sustainable changes to conditions in their lives, such as better housing, employment, and improved health.

THOUGHTS FOR CONSIDERATION

*Injustice happens when power is abused and people cannot
fully live the life that God has intended. Injustice results in
poverty, oppression and persons being marginalized by
society. It keeps people from living in harmony with God and
with each other (Haugen 1999).*

*The word "Shalom" often simply translated as "peace" has a
much broader meaning in the Hebrew context. It includes
peace, but also depicts social justice, well-being and prosperity.
It is a declaration of right-relationships between people and
between people and God.*

CHAPTER FIVE

ADDRESSING INJUSTICE

I met her in an African nation and was struck by the sadness in her eyes. She was part of an organization whose members were all HIV positive. Her story was one that could probably be repeated in many different places, but she's given me permission to share it whenever I think it will help someone else. The goal of her group was simply to make and sell paper maché items in the local market, and with the profits, buy food and items for those who were in later stages of AIDS. They would deliver food as they did home care visits.

I had an opportunity to accompany her on her rounds and was so touched as she handed the small bags of vegetables to those who were so sick. She also did small things around the house. She was, at that time, not yet a believer. Before my time with her was up, I felt led to ask her about her faith, and she told me how she'd been infected with HIV by her unfaithful husband. When she'd tried to thwart off his sexual advances, suspecting his unfaithfulness, he would beat her into submission. He later died from AIDS and now she was infected. When she returned home to her village, she shared her diagnosis with her pastor. He refused to allow her admission to church, but told her she could sit on the outside to listen to the sermon. She'd become bitter and rejected God.

That day, with tears, she told me that she really wanted to come back to the Lord, and she prayed a beautiful prayer of repentance and invited the Lord to reign in her life again. Her ministry has taken on many new dimensions now as she incorporates prayer into her home visits.

Although it is rare that a Christian would disagree that the Church should address issues of injustice, oppression, and evil, it is equally rare to find individuals who feel comfortable talking about what form that takes when it comes to individual or corporate action.

Often it seems, that though most believe it *should* be done, at some level they also believe that it is too big, too dangerous, too risky, or too complicated to be involved in justice issues and, therefore, back away from seeking to know what addressing injustice means.

In the world missions arena it becomes a conversation of being "apolitical" most often and staying away from anything that would endanger our own ability to stay in the country to which we are sent. We also try to avoid anything which would endanger those with whom we work. So we tend to avoid issues that have any political aura and back away from putting ourselves or others at risk, often at the encouragement of policies of sending agencies who would insist on that stance, and usually with good reason.

At times we use *cultural sensitivity* or "respecting the way of culture as an excuse to not address issues of injustice, especially those of gender inequality. We turn a blind eye to wife beating, verbal abuse, aberrant behaviors, and though it may be a prevalent practice of a particular culture, it is still unjust for the victim of the abuse. Alexander Solzhenitsyn in his Nobel speech for literature wrote,

> Everything which is further away, which does not threaten this very day to invade our threshold—with all its groans, its stifled cries, its destroyed lives, even if it involves millions of victims—this we consider on the whole to be perfectly bearable and of tolerable proportions (Solzhenitsyn, n. d.).

In some ways, for us who are far from an immediate injustice, such as HIV/AIDS or sexual trafficking, though it is bothersome, but not invading our daily threshold, we are not forced to deal with it. For those who live with these issues on their doorsteps it can become more difficult to avoid action. Or conversely, a certain numbing to the constancy of the issue may take over and again nothing is done.

Most likely, however, the main reason most of us don't respond, and the church is not actively engaged, is that we simply don't know what to do.

Forms of Justice

There are many different ways of looking at justice. There are different types of justice and different terminologies that can be used when speaking about justice. There is a *distributive* justice implying that everyone in a society should be on the same economic plane or get their fair share. Communism embraced this ideology with "equality of all" as one of its fundamental principles. Today it is commonly referred to as *economic justice*. There are organizations whose goal is to help balance the economic divides in poor populations through income generating programs and projects.

Justice is also referred to as *procedural*, allowing that persons have been treated fairly in the way that they have been dealt with. *Retributive* justice is the idea that people deserve to be treated in the same way they treat others.

Social Justice, a term which has become almost a buzz word in church and missions circles today, is more difficult to define. Secular definitions imply that social justice is concerned with equal access to resources necessary to life, such as health care, material goods, etc.

Social justice from a Christian perspective is concerned with the transformation of structures and institutions into a moral and ethical design that God intended so that all persons could experience wholeness in every aspect of their lives (Micah 6:8 , Isaiah 56:1, Matthew 3:15, Matthew 22:39 NIV).

Systemic and structural issues go deep and wide and long into the fabric of a society. They govern, provide policy, dictate morés and written and unwritten law. They are the filters that decide what will stand, what will be corrupt, who will receive what and how it will be received. In that they go deep, wide and long, change in structures and systems requires time, knowledge of the culture, the context, and the people. Change requires relationships built over time and usually are best led by persons of the cultures who truly understand the system. And of utmost importance, systemic transformation as God intends requires that the hearts of those who make up the systems and structures are turned to Christ.

When the church, its members and partners stand together, work together, care about community issues, and attack injustice together, their strength is doubled against injustice. Most successful interventions against injustice occur when numbers of people stand in unity together, relying on the power and guidance of the Holy Spirit.

Many Christians have begun to use the term *social justice* as a way of speaking about any compassion outreach, which is not a correct use of the term. Compassion outreach, according to Cannon (2009), responds to the effects of the problems of injustice. Social justice, on the other hand, addresses their systemic causes.

Thus far, the responses to issues and needs that have been presented in this text could be seen as levels of response: relief—the immediate, crisis-oriented, short-term response;

development—the long-term, ongoing, sustainable response; and now, social justice—the systemic response that looks at institutional and structural change.

Each of these responses may be appropriate for what is occurring in the context or setting of the need. The questions to be posed are, What response is appropriate for the one who is wishing to give assistance? What is the capacity, training, and willingness of the one who wishes to help? And, what do the people really want and need?

GOD HATES INJUSTICE AND WANTS IT TO STOP

It is clear from Scripture that God hates injustice and oppression (Psalm 11:5) and loves righteousness and justice (Psalms 11:7; 103:6), and desires that the chains of injustice be broken and the oppressed be set free. This is wonderfully stated in the following passage:

> Is not this the kind of fasting I have chosen: to loose the chains of injustice and untie the cords of the yoke, to set the oppressed free and break every yoke? Is it not to share your food with the hungry and to provide the poor wanderer with shelter—when you see the naked, to clothe him, and not to turn away from your own flesh and blood? Then your light will break forth like the dawn, and your healing will quickly appear; then your righteousness will go before you, and the glory of the LORD will be your rear guard (Isaiah 58:6–8, NIV).

INJUSTICE RESULTS IN UNTOLD SUFFERING THROUGHOUT THE WORLD

Injustice happens, according to Haugen (1999) of International Justice Mission, when power is abused and people are prevented from living life to the full as God has intended. Injustice results in poverty, oppression, and persons being marginalized by society. It prevents people from living in harmony with God and with each other. It prevents people from experiencing "shalom" at many levels of their lives (Gordon, 2003):

Individual level—wrongful imprisonment, trafficking, child labor, HIV contracted from an unfaithful spouse, etc.

Community level—land is wrongfully taken from a community, or a group is forced to leave its land, a group is denied access to education, or discriminated against as a group for some reason, etc.

State level—a group of people is denied access to their basic needs of food, shelter, health care, means of production, etc. because of corruption, or wrongful distribution of wealth and power.

Global level—large global institutions such as the World Bank or large governments make policies that negatively affect the poor, or contribute to corrupt governments knowing that funds are not getting to the people who need them (Gordon, 2003, p. 39).

Following is a brief look at some of the issues that are caused by injustice at some level of society, often stemming from the hearts of men and women which are evil and not reconciled with God, who are at top government levels and filtering down into all strata of society.

Malnutrition in Children

At the time of the writing of this book, one third of childhood deaths in the world are related to malnutrition. That infants and children do not have enough food or the right kinds of food to eat can be related to many different factors, but essential to them all is poverty. Poverty is a justice issue. Poverty is related to power and the distribution of wealth. As was pointed out in earlier chapters, it has many layers of complexity, but in those layers lie issues of injustice. That children cannot get enough to eat, in any society, in any nation, can never be referred to as justice and must always be addressed until Jesus comes.

That children cannot break out of a poverty cycle because they cannot think and learn because their brain cells are not nourished well enough to capture thoughts and retain them is simply not acceptable. It is not justice. Something in society has gone wrong and it is not an easy fix. Feeding children from the outside, though it may help, will never solve the problem of childhood deaths. It is intrinsically a problem that has to begin to be fixed "from the roots up" and from the top down, and really at every level in between.

HIV/AIDS

If AIDS comes from a virus and is sexually transmitted for the most part, how can it be connected with injustice? Much could be said about cultural injustices that disallow women to refuse sex with husbands that they know are unfaithful and who often bring HIV home to them. It seems unjust that that same wife-victim, then infects her newborn child at childbirth or through breast feeding. It seems unjust that in some cultures a husband would insist that his wife practice "dry sex," using herbs to make her vagina dry so that he would have more stimulation while she would be more subject to vaginal tears and more likely to contract the virus. It is unjust that because there are myths that say that having sex with a small child or virgin will cure AIDS, that men will buy or rape a child and also likely infect that child with HIV in order to try to cure himself. It seems so wrong that millions of children have lost one or both parents to the epidemic and often lose their rights to inheritance of property as well. Injustice abounds for those infected or affected by HIV/AIDS.

Politically, HIV/AIDS has huge justice implications as well. When large amounts of funding became available (or did not become available at first) governments began to vie for the funding, yet the funding wasn't always allocated to the HIV/AIDS issue (Moyo, 2009). It continued to be a political issue when governments, especially in highly epidemic areas, decided how much emphasis they would give it in their overall budget. It was a political issue when developed countries were deciding what in their aid budgets would go to health care in other countries. It became a huge (and positive) political issue when a United States President declared a fifteen billion dollar grant for AIDS in Africa, but then was dependent on Congress for its funding. It was a political issue when drug companies were asked to reduce the price for antiretroviral drugs that would prolong lives and at first refused to do so. And on and on it goes, leaving still a very large percentage of people without life-prolonging antiretroviral drugs, often for political reasons—a very political issue indeed.

GENDER INEQUALITIES

The inferior way in which women are viewed in many cultures has set up a series of injustices against women that are tragic to contemplate and seemingly overwhelming in scope. Recent media coverage of the atrocities of the prolonged war in the Democratic Republic of Congo (DRC) depicted the multiple rapes and mutilations of women by the invading soldiers and even by the peace-keeping military sent to prevent this sort of thing from occurring. This media coverage is finally bringing attention to this part of the world where for the last five or six years this tragedy has gone on without anyone seeming to notice. As Solzhenitsyn said, it was perfectly bearable for most of us as it wasn't a part of our daily threshold and not "in our face" until well-known personalities such as Hillary Clinton decided to make it a media story. And even though we now know about it, one has to wonder if anything has actually been done to lessen the incidence of its occurrence?

The issues of gender inequality have ramifications for so many of the issues of injustice—lack of education for women, inequality in employment opportunities, genital mutilation of women, the taking of property if widowed, nutritional issues as male children are given more food in some places, and on and on. Women in many cultures are the main producers of food and the caretakers of children, yet suffer the most injustice.

Human trafficking of women and children is a huge money making industry in the world today. It ranks among that of the sale of drugs and illegal weapons. Women and children are sold or trafficked against their will (or deceived) into some kind of labor or sex slavery or sex trade. Often they become the property of pimps or madams and have such high levels of indebtedness that there is little probability of breaking free from the prostituted life to which they have been enslaved.

They are often the victims of violence, exposed to all kinds of sexually transmitted diseases, often not permitted or are paid more not to use condoms to protect themselves. They are at high risk for contracting HIV. Children of the prostituted women, if not in the trade themselves, are also at risk to be exploited and are exposed to far more than any child should ever see. Many times they lie under the beds of their mothers while they work. Women and children who are prostituted are often given drugs and many become addicted at early ages.

Police may in some cases be part of the clientele, so protection for the women and children cannot be assumed or guaranteed. If for some reason the women and/or children do escape or are rescued, their families may not be willing to receive them back because of what they have been involved with or because they have become sick.

Female Genital Mutilation—In some cultures, it is a practice for young women to undergo an excision or mutilation of her clitoris and/or other parts of her female genitalia as she reaches puberty as part of a "rite of passage" before marriage. This is usually carried out in unsterile conditions, by someone improperly prepared to do surgical procedures. The incisions often leave scarring, may cause inabilities to urinate properly, difficulties with births, absence of sexual pleasure, and even difficulty in having sexual relations at all. The reasons behind this practice are many, but often have to do with assuring that a girl is a virgin before marriage and keeping her from straying once married.

The practice has been called to public attention in recent years, but is still carried out in at least twenty-eight countries. Young women who refuse to conform may be beaten, imprisoned, rejected for marriage, and ostracized by their peers. Those who speak out may even be put to death. Parents who do not wish to subject their daughters to this practice may find it hard to find anyone willing to pay a bride price and may also find themselves discriminated against in their own communities.

PERSONS WITH DISABILITIES

Persons with disabilities are among the most disadvantaged vulnerable groups in the world according to the World Health Organization. Widespread poverty, excessive inequality and flagrant abuse of their human rights are the major stumbling blocks to their development as equal citizens of their countries. See <http://www.who.int/topics/disabilities/en/>.

There is a cycle between poverty and disabilities. The poor are at greater risk for acquiring a disability due to lack of access to good nutrition, hygiene, health care as well as safe living and working conditions. Due to instability in governments, there is also a great increase in risk of being disabled due to riots, civil unrest and war. The numbers of people missing limbs and blinded by landmines in Cambodia, for example continues to increase, after all these years following the Khmer Rouge genocide.

In some places the injustices against persons with disabilities are unimaginable. Persons with severe mental or physical challenges are socially ostracized, hidden away, locked up, placed in institutions with deplorable conditions and inhuman treatment, degraded, exploited, at times even put to death or allowed to die, and there are no provisions made to make life workable for them at any level of society.

Though there are some organizations dedicated to speak up for the disabled, their influence and strength has not met the worldwide need. It seems that the church is well poised to be in a position of influence and voice to speak out against injustice against persons made in the image of God and loved and cherished by him in equal measure to any human being. Yet without intention, the church itself may actually create an injustice against persons with disabilities by their very exclusion socially and attitudinally from the heart and life of the Christian community.

GENOCIDES

Genocide is the deliberate and systematic destruction, in whole or in part, of an ethnic, racial, religious, or national group. It is often done for "ethnic cleansing" in a society or culture as was experienced in the Bosnian war. Tribal rivalry was the cause in Rwanda, when people who had lived side by side, but were of different tribal origins began to slaughter each other and over eight hundred thousand persons died. Another million were forced to flee the country to save their lives. Thousands more died as a result of cholera once they were in refugee camps in Zaire and Tanzania. This tragedy occurred in 1994 and it is reported that there are still those who suffer from Post Traumatic Stress Disorder as a result of having gone through this experience. Though reconciliation has reportedly occurred between the two tribes, the scars of that atrocity will remain for a long time to come.

The above are just brief summaries of some of the many injustices that occur on the worldwide scene. One could go on narrowing the list closer to home and to issues that affect the daily lives of the reader—pedophilia, child abuse in the home, spousal abuse, exploitation of students by teachers, corruption in court systems, corruption in police systems, etc. From the macro systems of the world to the everyday lives of humankind, injustice can be found.

The Church Responding to Injustice

In order to be faithful to what God would have for His people and in order to minister holistically, the Church—its saved, restored, reconciled, Spirit-filled, members—need to be involved in fighting injustice. It is biblical, it is Christian, it is right. Yet, the *how* remains illusive.

The word "shalom," often simply translated as "peace," has a much broader meaning in the Hebrew context. It includes peace, but also depicts social justice, well-being, and prosperity. It is a declaration of right relationships between people and God.

In Luke 4 (as discussed in chapter 1 of this book), Jesus is describing a state of shalom as he speaks of the "Year of Jubilee." This refers to the Old Testament's year of Jubilee when slaves were set free, debts forgiven, and land returned to its original owners. This was God's way of bringing balance to the economy and keeping the rich from getting too rich, and His way of creating justice for the poor.

God is calling the body of believers, His Church, to bring right relationship or justice to the poor and oppressed, and to right the injustices, especially those done to the poor.

Micah 6:8 (NIV) gives us a biblical basis for responses of compassion and justice: "He has showed you, O man, what is good. And what does the Lord require of you? To act justly and to love mercy and to walk humbly with your God."

The following are ways the Church can respond to injustice. These actions may be individuals who are part of the Church, it may be the church at large, it may be a group who is part of the church, and it may be a missionary entity sent by the church. However, it is felt that it is the Church that is called to action. It is the Church that is the voice of Jesus to its community and has the strongest voice to be heard when it comes to change from the roots up.

A. *Prayer.* All persons can commit to interceding on behalf of those who are suffering injustice. Prayer vigils, prayer walks, prayer groups, and intercessory prayer are all vital for these important issues to be turned around. Before any initiative or specific intervention is undertaken, directive prayer is essential. Ephesians 6 states that "Our struggle is not against flesh and blood, but against the rulers, against the authorities, against the powers of this dark world" (verse 12, NIV), and specific armor for spiritual battle is given and needed when taking up the fight against injustice. Very specific direction and guidance from the Lord will be needed and those going to fight injustice head on will need the power of the Holy Spirit and spiritual discernment to be present. This work cannot be done without prayer.

B. *Evangelism and Discipleship.* Spreading the good news of Jesus from Jerusalem to the ends of the earth is the mandate of the Church and certainly the mission of the Church. Changing hearts is the starting point in righting relationships and changing evil to good. Changed lives should equal changed communities and changed societies, but until Jesus returns and Satan is taken captive, evil will remain in the world and injustice will need to be fought. Though bringing people to Christ and spreading the good news is the foremost mission of the Church, it is not the only mission and not the only answer to the problem of evil that confronts the Church and the world.

Once people have come to Christ, they need to be strengthened and grounded in the knowledge of Him. Bible schools and ministerial training should include training on justice issues and training and encouragement for this to be part of the mandate of the Church.

C. *Compassionate Care.* It has been clearly pointed out that meeting in responsible ways the needs of those who are suffering is part of the mandate of the Church. *Retaining the dignity of individuals by enabling and empowering their capacity and helping people to help themselves is part of justice for the poor.* While strengthening the hands of the poor and giving voice to the voiceless by strengthening people and communities, there is greater possibility for people to stand up for themselves when injustice comes their way.

When the church and community stand together, work together, care about community issues, and attack injustice together, their strength is doubled against injustice. Most successful interventions against injustice occur when numbers of people stand in unity together.

When compassionate care is administered in holistic fashion as mentioned in earlier chapters and Kingdom values are upheld and the love of Jesus communicated, relationships are infused with a new dimension of understanding. A unity of heart and Spirit-anointing from above take on the supernatural ability to stand against the evils that prevail.

D. *Becoming the Voice for Voiceless.* The church is well-positioned to become an advocate for any persons or groups who have been marginalized or rendered voiceless by some means. These types of persons abound, but examples would include widows and orphans, immigrants, persons, displaced and those with disabilities. The ministry of Christ and the ministry of the church is that of reconciliation. It is one of breaking down the walls between church and community—the walls that would separate church from neighbor as has been stated in earlier chapters. By our inclusion of those who are voiceless, a very large wall is taken down and our welcoming attitude *of all who come* creates the safe harbor that Jesus intended the church to be. If reconciliation and healing are to happen, these groups of people must be able to *come inside the walls* and if they cannot come, the church must go to them.

Persons with disabilities are often not made to feel welcome for example. One of the first steps in advocacy is the very inclusion of the disabled into the life of the church. By making small changes even in building structures so that wheelchair access and other accessibility issues can be accomplished is a statement of welcome and acceptance to the church community. The church can also be sure that persons with hearing and visual impairments have provisions during the service so that they can enter into worship. An attitude of open arms and acceptance speaks to the community and to families that these are people of value to the community of believers and to God; people to be included in the life of the church. Persons of influence politically in the church can lobby for equal opportunities, and the church can join together in these types of policy decisions that make life better for those with disabilities.

Persons who have been displaced often lose hope very quickly as all that is familiar has been taken away, often without warning a person, family or community's life can be completely turned upside down. It is the perfect opportunity for the church to be the church by offering comfort, guidance, tangible assistance and welcoming arms into the body of Christ.

Immigrants as well are often seeking a new start, a new life and the church. The church can reach out by offering assistance with job hunting, visa and registration issues, material needs, etc.

The Bible is clear about the church's responsibility to care for the widows and orphans (James 1:27). There are many practical ways that the church can assess and then respond to the needs that a widow may have. Sometimes the biggest challenge facing the widow is just having help with household "fix it" jobs or dealing with a vehicle. Orphans, in the US may have opportunities for fostering and other forms of welfare, but in many places of the world, this is not the case. Finding ways to place children in Christian homes where they learn not only family values but what it means to have Christ as Savior is a valuable contribution the church can make.

If persons without voice are in any way excluded from the body of Christ, it would seem that according to the Scripture, the body is not complete (1 Cor. 12.12).

E. *Relationship Building at Community Levels.* In order to have influence over issues that matter and ultimately over justice issues, it is imperative that Christians and the local church have relationships with decision makers and ultimately become decision makers. When the church and community are in good relationship and begin working together on projects for the betterment of the community, good relationships with community leaders are bound to occur. Eventually Christians are going to begin to take positions of leadership within the community structures. This begins to give voice to decisions which positively affect justice issues at a local level and ultimately can begin to affect decisions at upper levels of policy makers.

An example of this is a pastor of a local church in Zambia whose church began an HIV/AIDS program of testing and counseling for HIV for the local community. It was so appreciated and became noticed because one of the persons who came for help was related to a politician. The politician notified the newspaper which did a story on the church. The television network then came to do an interview. Funding became available and the program grew. Eventually the pastor was asked to serve on a government committee for HIV/AIDS. Over the years he was asked to chair that committee. He now chairs the national committee for HIV/AIDS and sits on the President's Cabinet. He continues to pastor his church and has great influence in his local community and the capital city. He speaks at conferences worldwide, but remains a humble servant of the Lord.

Before genuine relationships between church and community can be formed, true reconciliation and transformation between brothers and sisters within church walls must be happening. Racial barriers, animosities, church politics, and all that goes into inner church strife will not make the church an effective witness outside its walls.

F. *Political Activity*. Christians and churches tend to shy away from the political arena because of its known corruption and the fear of having to compromise too much to be a part of that system. On the other hand, if we have no Christians in government, decisions that are made will become further and further away from the morals and standards that would uphold justice. Jesus challenged the political practices of his time. He kicked people out of the temple. He didn't sit back and just allow things to happen. By not becoming involved, as Gordon (2003) says, we are making a political decision, to allow injustice to continue. Political action can take many forms:

1. Get to know the congressperson and actively engage with them over agendas that the church knows to be right.

2. Encourage our Christian young people to be involved in politics and legal action and take up careers along these lines so that we have Christians in the political arenas.

3. Know the platforms of those who are running for office and vote split ballots and support those who are standing up for agendas that will support justice.

4. In foreign settings, know the risks involved in encouraging political activity among nationals and be prayerful about what involvement should be and what outcomes one is willing to endure.

5. Be careful not to endanger the lives of those who have to stay in a foreign setting but not cop out of

encouraging political activism of others if injustice is rampant. The Church must have a voice in injustice.

G. *Partner with Organizations That Know What to Do.*
There are organizations that have specific goals to deal with some of the injustices that have been listed above. One such organization is the International Justice Mission. This is a Christian human rights agency that secures justice for victims of slavery, sexual exploitation and other forms of violent oppression. International Justice Mission lawyers, investigators, and after-care professionals work with local officials to ensure immediate victim rescue and after-care, to prosecute perpetrators and to promote functioning public justice systems.

The Assemblies of God also has an organization, Project Rescue, which has been helping rescue and restore women and children who have been sold into sexual slavery and helping them to find new life in Christ. They and several other organizations have developed an after-care curriculum which gives guidance in helping victimized and battered women find a way to put their lives back together and move on to a meaningful, productive, and quality life.

The Salvation Army for many years has been doing excellent work with the issue of human trafficking and has developed many resources and networks to deal with this issue. Several agencies have formed an alliance and are working together to address the trafficking issue.

Though it is wise for the church to consult with and utilize the resources of the agencies and organizations which have experience with these issues, it is also a tendency to hand the work over to them and step back and allow them to take over.

It is my belief that it is the responsibility of all the Church, using all our hands, our hearts and our resources, to partner together with the power of the Holy Spirit functioning in us to work, to fight, to pray, to do spiritual battle against injustice so that shalom may come and so that peace on earth may be experienced by more and more until Jesus comes.

I would wish that injustice would be intolerable for us all even if it is not at our doorstep.

THOUGHTS FOR CONSIDERATION

Relief says that we should give clothes to someone who needs them. But justice says that we must not take jobs away from people who would make clothes. Justice says that we should invest in textile businesses that would employ people and provide clothes at a reasonable price.

Justice looks at systems that cause oppression and poverty, and tries to develop long-term solutions. Justice is not just concerned with meeting immediate needs, but with creating dignity. Justice says that 'helping' people sometimes causes more harm than good (Conrad, 2010)

Chapter Six

Donor Dilemmas & "Best Practice in Missions"

The missionary hung up the phone after talking to one of her large supporting churches. The church wants to come to her field of service and "build an orphanage." They know that there are many AIDS orphans having visited her field one time and noted the street children. They have also gleaned the plight of the orphans from her newsletters. She didn't know what to say. She knew that orphanages were not the best practice for dealing with orphaned children. She'd read all the literature and studies that said institutionalizing children, especially when done by foreigners or those outside the culture, would cause identity issues for the children. They would lose grip on their cultural heritage. She knew that they would be at risk for exploitation within the orphanage by older children or orphanage workers. She knew that no matter how hard she tried, she could never replicate a normal family or teach family values. She knew the kids would be at risk for communicable disease and that when they left the institution they would not be prepared to cope with life in their culture and they would have no family to return to. She also knew that it would cost 14 to 16 times more to put children in an institution than in a family and she had no means of continuing that kind of support nor would the national church with whom she worked.

But, knowing all of that and knowing it was not best practice and not in the best interest of the children, could she really say no to the donor? Would they cut off her support if she didn't abide by their wishes? Would they understand if she tried to tell them some of these principles? Would they accept an alternative?

There were other questions too. Just because these were her beliefs about best practice, were those beliefs really shared by the national church? Would they be more inclined to accept outside help if she weren't in the middle? If she said no to this donor, would it be fair to the church she was working with in that they might be able to get something out of it?

Then there was that nagging question that was always at the back of her mind: "What about her own lifestyle?" Here she was saying an institution wasn't an appropriate way to deal with orphans and some of these poor little kids were out on the streets or living in horrid situations while she had her own comfortable space, plenty of it really, without any extra folk living with her. She had all the food and comforts she needed and lived with security guards and lots of things to keep her in touch with home. She lived the way she was more or less accustomed to live. Was it right? Was it too much? She'd talked to the local church leaders about it and they assured her that it was fine with them, but were they really being honest?

Those questions kept her awake at night and have kept many missionaries and nationals awake as they have pondered these and other questions as well as the "donor dilemma." What does one do if the right or best practice for the recipient conflicts with the wishes and interests of the donor? What should be done? Is there a satisfactory answer that can balance the wishes of the donor with the needs being met and "best practice" being carried out?

DONOR EXPECTATIONS

The donors saw a need. They visited, they heard, they felt and their hearts were moved. They knew that children were homeless and that they had lost their parents. The paradigm that they know is that when children lose their parents in other countries (not the USA any longer, interestingly), an orphanage seems to be what is done. Since constructing buildings in other countries is something that the USA church has become proficient at doing, and raising funds to house orphans is relatively easy money to come up with, the US donor church feels compelled to act on what they have seen and what they know historically to be true. Probably they have not done extensive research on what the literature says about what is best for orphans or what the international communities and many large NGOs and governments are now doing for orphans. They simply had a meeting and decided what to do. Thus the phone call. The donor wheels are in motion.

Since the donor is the donor, there is an expectation on the part of the donor that there should be a certain amount of directive ability in how the funds are used since they are in fact coming up with the funds. They also think that they are functioning in the best interest of everyone: the children, the church, and the missionary. Why would they have reason to think otherwise, when, this is how it's been in the past?

Thus the donor expectation—they hear about, are told about, have a revelation about, or sense a need. They decide to respond. They rally support for the need and volunteerism and/or finances result. They direct the way in which the funds will be used and expect to see the results of their effort so that they can report back that what they said they were going to do, they in fact did. These are not unrealistic expectations.

THE LOCAL CHURCH IN THE FIELD

The church really does want to be a hand extended to its community. It believes that ministry to the whole person means just that and truly wants to be a lighthouse in meeting social, physical, and emotional needs of its own and of those in the community around it. But the offerings only go so far. Yes, the church does have assets beyond money, but the volunteers are already doing so much. The HIV/AIDS crisis has really taken a toll on the resources. Reaching out to the AIDS orphans is really a stretch for the church. There is a sense that something should be done, but *what* and *with what* are questions that need to be answered. Every family seems to be taxed already with extra children, and financially, they couldn't take in more without help.

The church knows the dangers of accepting too much outside assistance, but the temptation is there to grab whatever is offered and worry about undoing any entanglement or dependency later. It keeps the pastors awake at night wondering about what is right and best for all involved.

Is there a way that one can bring balance to involve people "from the roots up" in solving their own problems, and still provide ways in which partnerships with donors can occur in responsible and healthy ways? Are there ways for donors to provide for needs yet not build dependencies? Are there ways for donors to help that also do not create unhealthy and poor practices that will never be sustainable by the people who need them? Is there a way for missionaries to be an equal part of the partnership with national churches?

Does Aid Help?

In a thought-provoking book entitled, Dead Aid (2009), Dambisa Moyo, a Harvard-educated Zambian economy student who grew up in Africa, examines the problem of government aid to the continent from a historical and modern day prospective. She points out the dismal failure of the billions of dollars of governmental aid over the last fifty years that has been given to Africa. She demonstrates the inability of that aid to solve Africa's poverty and economic issues. Conversely, she feels that the aid has actually crippled Africa's ability to get on its feet and solve its own problems because it has created so much corruption of leaders and so much dependency that there has been little reason or motivation for Africa to make Africa work. She begs for personalities like Bono, Oprah, Gates, and others to step aside, keep their money at home and allow Africa to get itself on its feet.

Though extreme in her views, Moyo (2009) makes some excellent points. She quotes Rwanda's President Kagame in a Time Magazine interview in 2007 as saying,

> The donors (having put 400 billion dollars into Africa) have made a lot of mistakes. Many times they have assumed that they are the ones who know what countries in Africa need. They want to be the ones to choose where to put this money, to be the ones to run it, without any accountability. In other cases they have just associated with the wrong people and money gets lost and ends up in people's pockets. We should correct that (p. 48).

Those who have traveled around the world have no doubt observed, as have I, the many pieces of farm equipment rusting in the fields. Tractors and earth-moving equipment of every kind are simply sitting where they broke down, with no chance of ever moving from that spot. Whether it was ever needed in the first place is doubtful. Whether it did harm to the soil it rolled over is probable. Whether anyone gave thought, when it was donated, to how it would be repaired, how parts would be obtained and how fuel would be afforded, is improbable. So often donations have been ill-thought through and given, perhaps with good intentions, but not always very wisely.

Someone wakes in the night, with a "God told me" moment. Without doing proper research, checking into "best practice" or good development principles, without knowing what might be best for the people or the place or the country of the intended donation, they simply begin to ignite enthusiasm around them. If they are dynamic personalities and great communicators, they have a good chance of raising the funds or whatever it is they are trying to amass, and thus, rusting tractors sit in fields.

Then there are the handouts or gifts every time the missionary or foreigner appears on the scene in an unreached or new place. Buying favor in a new place sets up a difficult scenario for a long-term relationship with a group of people. For example, when a missionary wants to form a relationship with an unreached tribe in a remote location, he brings gifts for each person each time he visits. When the next group that he asks to come visits, he asks them to be sure to bring a gift for everyone. When they were reluctant, his response was, "You have to; they expect it." Being generous is always a good thing, but there is also a fine line between buying one's way into favor and relationship and simply wanting to bless people with something that they need and want.

It would seem that when entering any new community, wisdom would say not to start with handouts, but to wait and form relationships and then see how one can best help with the

guidance of those who will receive. If one is going to bless, bless
well. It appears in the above examples, the following is true:
Donations given to the recipients were not part of the decision-
making process about what they needed. The "roots up" or
local ideas were not considered. Assessments were not done to
determine the assets and needs. Best practice was not
thoroughly processed. Lack of accountability could have
allowed corruption to flourish.

DOING GIVING WELL—A BALANCING ACT

The intent of this chapter is not to discourage donors from
giving, or recipients from receiving. As a missionary dependent
on funding for my livelihood, it would be foolish to advocate
this view. The intent, rather, is to examine what constitutes
solid missions practice. It is also to view donor needs and
expectations and to see if there may be a balance that can be
reached between both, with satisfactory outcomes that will be
of the most benefit for the Kingdom of God. And most
importantly is to ascertain that the recipients will also receive a
sustainable benefit that they in fact need and want.

Look at the progression of what has been discussed in this
book thus far:

- A biblical approach is ministry to the whole person.

- Ministering in word and deed is an integrated approach
  to mission and ministry.

- Believing in each person's ability to help themselves and to bring something to the equation affords dignity and respect to all. Therefore not doing for but with allows solutions to arise from the "roots up."

- The local church (on the field) is the best agent to transform the community with one of the roles of the church to care for its own and those around them.

- Transformational development is a tool that allows for sustainable change over time working in and through the local church—and thereby, not creating dependency—and being able to replicate what is learned.

- The responsibility of the church is to address the issues of injustice and to speak loudly and clearly against injustice and to be involved in actively engaging in trying to right wrongs.

- The Holy Spirit brings power, anointing, insight, and unifying ability to surpass many of the natural barriers towards righting injustice and gives the body of Christ a voice in otherwise voiceless situations.

If all of those principles are accepted as true, then good missiological practice would say that a missionary would be working in partnership with the local church. Together they would, as the Holy Spirit guides and enables, establish goals and ministries that would meet the vision that the church and its members have for reaching the lost and touching its community with healing and transformation.

It would seem that the onus first and foremost for defining what is needed from outside donors would be on the missionary and local church body. If nothing has been thought through to present to the donor, then when such a call comes, and the donor already has a project in mind, a dilemma occurs for both.

However, if, for example, there is a large issue with AIDS orphans, the first step it would seem would be for the local missionary and church to get together for prayer and dialogue as to what might be some reasonable solutions and steps to begin to address this need. Is it the vision and burden of the church and mission to begin to address the issue of AIDS orphans? Is God speaking this to their hearts? Are there those in the congregation and in the mission who feel it strongly enough to be the champions and give of their time and resources to be the lead people and who are willing to step up and organize the efforts?

Obviously the missionary in this case has already done some research about the issue of orphanages and can bring that information to the table. She has found in her research and assessment what is happening around the country and other models of caring for AIDS orphaned children that she presents as part of the discussion:

- Assistance to child-headed households by church offerings, small micro-enterprises, or grants

- Assistance to church families willing to take a child into their homes

- Setting up a para-church fostering program, organized and run by a church committee, and operated by a small micro-enterprise or grant

- Setting up a church-based group home housing eight to ten children with a Christian house parent or parents, perhaps from the church.

An asset assessment could be done (refer to Chapter 7).

Once a plan is decided upon, a budget would be drawn up. As part of that budget, one could put in one-time gifts from outside donors.

It is rarely wise to build any kind of ongoing programmatic expenses based on outside funding, such as a church or individual donor, as their continuance cannot be assured. Doing this does not set up a sustainable, replicable model. Donor funds are well-used for capital expenses such as buildings, or investing in a small business. This doesn't build an ongoing dependency. If a donor will be committed over time, there could be an end-point where that funding will no longer be needed, perhaps in five years, and the program will by then be sustainable.

Once a plan is established, the missionary and/or church is ready for the donor. Ready to say, "Well, we really don't want to do an orphanage for these reasons, but we think we have a better plan to help our orphans. And we believe there is a significant role that you can play." They might suggest, "Would you be willing to come and build a group home?" Or, "Would you be willing to fund a small bakery so our kids could learn to bake bread, and so we could have an ongoing way to support the families that are taking in AIDS orphans, etc.?" Most of the time, donors are willing to change their method as long as it is somewhat related to what they wanted to originally do.

The point being if the recipients have planned well and are ready for the donors and have a reasonably good and exciting venture in which the donors can be involved and feel that they are investing in something worthwhile and something tangible, they most often will want to participate and will feel that their expectations are being met.

Often, when donors realize that they can invest in something that will keep on going—like a micro-enterprise such as the small bakery mentioned above, that will not only teach a vocational skill, but will help to fund a few families to care for orphans—they find this to be a great way for their missions money to be used. They see that it will continue to serve others for a long time and not just stop with a structure or one-time project.

SUPPORT OF PASTORS OR LOCAL CHURCHES

There are a number of differing opinions on what the indigenous church really means. As explained in an early chapter, this text defines it to mean a church which has become self-supporting, self-governing, and self-propagating. These are not just words, nor principles, but are biblical principles based on a model put forth by the New Testament Church.

The reason that the support of a pastor by outside entities is discouraged is directly related to the encouragement of the local body to bring their "tithes and offerings into the storehouse" (Malachi 3:10) as commanded by Scripture and to support their pastor as their shepherd. Once a church realizes that their pastor receives finances from someone else, they have little motivation to follow the biblical mandate to work toward doing that themselves.

When national believers do not support their own pastors, the impression is reinforced that Christianity is a foreign religion that has neither taken root nor inspired the commitment of its followers. Furthermore, church members can resent a pastor who is not accountable to them because his salary is paid by a foreign mission or church. This danger is especially great today, as some North American churches have started directly supporting pastors of poorer churches overseas, bypassing the local congregations those pastors serve (Ott, 1993).

On the other hand, it is a tremendous testimony of love and commitment when national believers who have so little sacrifice to support their own pastors or send evangelists to tell others the Good News. This demonstrates that Christianity is not a Western religion or an agent of imperialism, but has in fact commanded the deepest commitments among the various peoples of the earth (Ott, 1993).

Likewise, the support of local churches comes into discussion. True, it does seem that the responsibility of a church, no matter the size and the struggle, is to support its own shepherd. But where does one draw the line in giving assistance to a church? Is it okay to build a building for a church while not okay to support its programs or pastor? Who and how has all of this been determined? A one-time gift is determined to be okay as it doesn't build dependency, but ongoing programmatic expenses do—a reasonable conclusion.

I believe that most outside churches desire to truly help. They want to extend their borders and witness to "the uttermost parts" and want to do it in the most effective Kingdom manner. In most cases, there is simply not an educational process in place that assists missionaries, national churches or outside churches to know the most appropriate intervention strategies. Thus the writing of this book is an attempt to begin to raise awareness of some of these issues.

WHAT TO DO WITH AN EXISTING PROJECT OR PROGRAM THAT IS NOT THE BEST PRACTICE

Often, practitioners of one type of another end up inheriting a ministry, a compassionate outreach of some sort, that may not be the best practice. Having read this book, one may be thinking that the likelihood of sustainability is improbable, that there is little or no local church involvement, that it is missionary driven, or that it is definitely dependent on outside funds or personnel. What does one do in that situation?

Many people do find themselves in exactly that situation. Sometimes paradigms change and the way things were done in one paradigm is no longer considered to be the best way to do things in the new wave of thinking.

Armed with new knowledge, the practitioner can begin to assess the ministry's value to those who are receiving whatever it is offering and certainly begin to involve the recipients of the ministry in that assessment. In many countries where orphanages, for example, were at one time considered the right way to care for abandoned or orphaned children, some organizations are beginning to look for ways of fostering the children out of the institutions and gradually closing them. Others are finding ways to restructure the institution into more modular, family-like units and incorporating local mom and dad type caregivers, trying to create the best family atmosphere that can be done in that type of setting. Others are doing group homes and having eight to ten children in a home with a Christian mom and/or dad and having the church help to support the family as an extension of the church's ministry.

The main thing is to do the best that can be done and work toward making it as good as can be under the circumstances. In due time, you must try to educate and inspire others around you toward a different approach and set some goals to begin transitioning if it is feasible.

In a thought provoking article by Conrad (2010), he shares the following:

- Churches are talking about AIDS, hunger, education, and micro-enterprise. Thousands of American Christians travel to Africa each year to love and serve people who have been forgotten and marginalized for decades.

- I have come to realize that many of the things that we do to help the poor may actually do more harm than good. In our efforts to love and serve people, it is easy to

create unhealthy dependency, and even to hinder
people's ability to work and provide for themselves.

- I am learning that there is a place for mercy—giving
  help to people for immediate needs. But mercy is not
  enough. We must also seek after justice—to help create
  systems and structures that allow people to live with
  dignity and provide for themselves.

- Let me share a story that may help illustrate. The first
  time I visited Africa, I was amazed that just about every
  man that we passed on the street was wearing an
  American t-shirt. I saw football jerseys, t-shirts from
  golf benefits, college t-shirts, and countless other shirts
  that had been made in the US, worn a couple of times,
  and then donated to charity.

- My first thought was that this was a great and simple
  way for Westerners to provide help and support for
  folks in Africa. We didn't need the shirts, and
  apparently people here did. Then I had a conversation
  with a friend who had lived in sub-Saharan Africa for
  many years. He told me that the endless donations of
  shirts had actually severely damaged the textile industry
  in Africa. Business can't compete with free shirts. So, an
  industry which could employ thousands of people in
  this part of the world simply doesn't exist.

- Mercy says that we should give clothes to someone who
  needs them. But justice says that we must not take jobs
  away from people who would make clothes. Justice says
  that we should invest in textile businesses that would

employ people and provide clothes at a reasonable price.

- Justice looks at systems that cause oppression and poverty, and tries to develop long-term solutions. Justice is not just concerned with meeting immediate needs, but with creating dignity. Justice says that *helping* people sometimes causes more harm than good.

- At the risk of dampening the enthusiasm that has begun to develop, I would suggest that the way Christians engage with issues of poverty must mature and change. While affirming the desire to reach out and help people, I propose that there is a next step to be taken.

- What is the next step? It is a movement from addressing immediate needs toward addressing systems and structures that cause poverty. It is a movement from doing things ourselves to equipping people to live. It is a movement from mercy to justice.

THOUGHTS FOR CONSIDERATION

*Partnership rests upon a foundation of mutual respect and
warm personal relationships. There must be ongoing love,
prayer, and fellowship. In short, unless genuine and abiding
friendship develops between the partners, their relationship
cannot hope to achieve the goals for which it was formed
(York, 2000, p. 158).*

*The only man who behaves sensibly is my tailor; he takes my
measurements anew every time he sees me, while all the rest
go on with their old measurements and expect me to fit them
(George Barnard Shaw).*

CHAPTER SEVEN

FIGURING IT OUT: ASSESSMENT & EVALUATION

Being labeled "latrine queen" may not be a very enviable title, but probably a well-earned one, as I was often heard speaking and nearly preaching on the importance of everyone having, using and cleaning a pit-latrine. This was the available sanitation in the area of the Democratic Republic of Congo (DRC) where I lived. Perhaps if I actually had to dig that six-meter hole myself, cut down the trees to make the walls, and gather the right kind of leaves for the thatching on the roof, I wouldn't have been quite so adamant. My public health self saw it as what just had to happen if we were ever going to get a handle on diarrhea and parasites.

A colleague in a neighboring country related an incident that underscores the importance of what will be discussed in this chapter: the need to really figure out what's happening and what needs to happen before embarking on assistance in other cultures.

This missionary was concerned with the high incidence of diarrhea in her area of service. She noted that there were no latrines in the village where this was occurring and saw that people seemed to do their toileting behind bushes and trees. She was sure that latrines would greatly cut down the incidence of diarrhea. When no one heeded her appeals, she went to the chief and explained the importance of latrines. She told him it would no doubt save the lives of many children. She offered to pay for the cost of the fuel to carry people to cut the trees necessary for the construction. The chief ordered it done and said there would be a fine imposed on any household that did not comply. The missionary was glad. She was happier when she saw the latrines constructed throughout the village.

Interestingly, the incidence of diarrhea remained unchanged. She couldn't understand it. One day she stopped in and asked to use one of the latrines and was amazed to find it fresh and clean. She could tell it had never actually been used. She began to inspect others and found the same. She went back to the chief and finally in a very embarrassed way, he admitted that it was a belief of his people that it was unhealthy and wrong to defecate in the same place twice. He didn't want to offend her by telling her that and he thought maybe when the latrines were built people would actually use them, but he could see that he was wrong.

The above example didn't actually harm anyone and is in fact somewhat amusing, but time, energy and money were lost as a result of lack of understanding. At times, however, not taking the time to adequately assess what is happening and what needs to happen can cause a negative consequence. Below are examples of a few documented incidents or practices that did not have the intended outcome:

Paying for the release of trafficked women. Some organizations in the early days of their attempts to rescue women and children trafficked into sex slavery in brothels, offered to pay their indebtedness for their release. Once the pimps and madams got the drift of this, they just upped the prices and were then able to purchase more trafficked women and children with the money they received. (These organizations soon realized this and changed their strategy of rescue.)

Formula and bottles for HIV positive women. In some areas, HIV positive women are advised not to breastfeed to reduce the risk of transmitting HIV to their infant. They are given a bottle and formula. In one place, a pile of baby bottles and cans of formula were found, discarded by the women soon after leaving the clinic. When asked why, it was found that those using bottles and formula were immediately identified as HIV positive and the stigma was just too much for the women.

Giving to beggars. Most people, especially at first exposure to street beggars in poorer countries, feel inclined to drop some coins or even more. Often the infants or children on the street will tug at most heartstrings and bring a response. Most who write on this subject advise against giving to street beggars, especially those with children, as the money made by just one generous donation of a tourist may be far more than could be earned in other ways. Therefore putting the child in school or in a healthier environment would not be considered due to the lucrative nature of the begging trade. There have also been reports of infants being intentionally maimed or disfigured to elicit more sympathy and therefore more money.

Issues with food and feeding. One report told of a mother who deprived her child to keep him underweight so that he would continue to qualify for the food supplement given at a feeding center. It was found that she used it for the rest of the family. Others have refused to eat certain relief foods if they note dates on the packaging that seem like expiration dates but are not. Others won't eat supplements that are associated with refugees as they don't want that same association.

Donations of Clothing. Donating clothes to other countries seems a good thing to do. In almost any place in the world, one can see people wearing western clothes and T-shirts from any organization under the sun. But what one doesn't realize is how the low cost of these donated goods has, in so many cases, undercut the ability of local textile industries to sell their own products locally. This also affects local seamstresses and tailors trying to make a living in their own settings. What seems like a good intention actually has negative consequences on a local economy.

These are just a few of the issues and negative consequences that can occur when cultural issues are not well understood.

These consequences are much more likely to happen when outsiders undertake interventions without participation of those they are trying to assist or at least without church or community participation.

How then can a missionary or a development worker, an outsider so to speak, figure out how to help, how to share in need, and how to best utilize the resources that may be available for assistance? As described in earlier chapters, persons from the outside, when confronted with need and who have more, with the best intentions and with the biblical mandate to have pity on those in need, really want to do something to help. How does one figure out what is happening and what needs to be done?

BEGINNING DIALOGUE

Chapter 2, "What Do People Really Want," stated that to begin dialogue with people that is effective and meaningful, it is necessary for trust to exist. That very statement implies that some sort of relationship needs to exist if trust is to be established. If the person entering the dialogue is a missionary, then likely time will be spent in simply building relationships with persons in the local church or targeted community and/or the population that will be served. If an outside entity, such as a USA church, is desirous to help, they may be able to come alongside a missionary or group who has already established trust and a relationship and covered much of what will be described in the following paragraphs. Without, however, someone taking the time to truly figure out what is happening and what needs to happen, time, funds and effort may be wasted and/or the most effective and sustainable result may not be obtained.

Because of the importance of trust in the process of transformational development and persons from different cultures working together, Covey's (2009) list of necessary ingredients for trust to occur will be listed again. People begin to trust individuals, groups and churches when they see:

- Consistency
- Integrity at every strata of interaction
- Honesty
- Follow-through
- Results
- True caring (which becomes evident over time as trust is established)

The word "partnership" has long been used to describe the relationship between the outside entity—the missionary and the church from the West—and national church. This is often referred to as the North coming to the South, but this nomenclature is no longer fitting as people send and receive from all parts of the world in these times. The late John York, theologian and missiologist of the Assemblies of God on partnership stated,

> Partnership rests upon a foundation of mutual respect and warm personal relationships. There must be ongoing love, prayer, and fellowship. In short, unless genuine and abiding friendship develops between the partners, their relationship

cannot hope to achieve the goals for which it was formed. (York, 2000, p. 158)

Ivan Satyavrata (2009), an Indian scholar, pastor and professor, in a lecture given to seminary students, extracts from Dr. York's thoughts on partnership the phrase "genuine and abiding friendship" and says,

> Friends share what they learn; friends open their hearts and minds to each other without secrecy. True friends allow the other to see right in and know them as they really are. True friends are eager to help and to spend ourselves for the other without counting the cost (p. 23).

True friendship, sees the importance of taking the time to work through the process of figuring out what is happening. Friends would care enough to want those involved to participate together in the process. Friends would be as concerned with the process and what can be learned from each other along the way as with the outcome. Friends find ways to share equally without domination, control and dependency happening in the process.

Much has been written about the difficulties of maintaining true partnerships between *haves* and *haves not* entities, especially because it is usually the *haves* that comes with and controls the funding and who thereby has the power. One could apply this to missionary/national relationships in many instances, as well. If one truly approaches these relationships as friendships, looking out for the good of each other, there may be a possibility of mutual trust developing more quickly.

Naturally there have been instances when those from the giving side have handed funds over to the recipients and the funds have not been used for what was intended, or the funds got diverted or even ended up in someone's pocket. Having that experience can cause a donor to say, "I have to be in control of the funds at all times." Funds can be the culprit of many partnerships' and friendships' dissolutions. The suggestion of the processes, which will be described in the following paragraphs, is to keep funding as a very low priority in all that will be discussed.

Keep this in mind, however. When a person from the outside, from a more developed country comes to a less developed one, from a place of have to a place of have less, there will most always be an expectation that the person or group from the outside has something to give that is not presently available. That is why it is always necessary to question the value of the outsider in the process. At times, the very presence of a foreign entity may derail an important self-discovery process just because there is an automatic expectation that everyone will somehow gain because that person or outside group is in the mix.

Depending on the situation and the nature of the relationship, that very issue may need to be a point of early discussion once a relationship is formed and a direction decided upon. Friends don't have secrets and it would be best to declare what the intention of giving or help might be—or not be—so that the expectations are not unrealistic.

CHURCH OR COMMUNITY DIALOGUE

Once relationships have been established with church or community leaders and it is clear that there is interest at leadership levels to address certain social issues, then a meeting to begin to engage others and build ownership is important. Church or community dialogue is a conversation that can take many forms. It can be multiple meetings with small groups or a large congregational meeting of many people together. Often the most successful meetings are those that are broken into separate gender groups, younger and older, etc., due to cultural issues of who can speak in front of whom, etc. The local leaders will know the best ways to approach these dialogue meetings.

It is important to have some key questions and participatory activities in mind for the meetings to ascertain if there is interest, willingness to participate and to elicit suggestions from the group as to how the problem might be addressed. It is also necessary to determine some objectives that are desired as a result of the meeting. The initial meetings are about awareness and discussion. Whatever information comes from the meeting will be useful, but the intent is simply to begin to introduce the subject and get people talking about it.

Some introductory discussion questions for an opening dialogue session may include:

1. What makes you proud to be a member of your community?

2. What characteristics are found in a healthy community?

3. What groups work together to make the community healthier?

4. What problems exist in your community?
   (A powerful way to address these issues, especially in rural communities and that will work with a small group, is to ask people to go outside and find an item on the ground that represents a problem in their community and bring it back to the meeting. An individual may bring an empty beer bottle, trash, or dirty water in a can (represents malaria or mosquitoes). Afterwards, have someone bring their item to the front to explain what it represents. The group can move the items around and vote on their priority. The issue you want to address may not be chosen. For example, if you think HIV/AIDS is a problem, find out why it was not identified.

5. What can be done about this problem? (If a priority item is identified, this may form the basis of ideas from the group to discuss how this issue might be addressed.)

6. Have you given thought to the problem of
   _____? (Fill in the blank.) This can introduce the issue not yet expressed, but may be deemed important to the church/community leaders and the missionary. It may become evident in these initial dialogue meetings when the groups do not have real interest in the issue or do not see it as priority. This may prompt a need to rethink what the likelihood of ownership and involvement would be if no one sees the issue as a problem. At times, the issues of priority to the people will need to be addressed first. In the course of

relationship building and the process, the issue of importance to the outsider may be introduced with education about the issue. It may or may not become something the group is willing to participate in. This is vital to the success and sustainability of any efforts put forth.

7. What could you personally do to be a part of the solution?

8. Would you be willing to work together to solve this problem?

These types of meetings can get people talking together and can generate excitement about what people can do for themselves. Depending on the culture, expectations and relationships established may be better served by local facilitators rather than outsiders for this type of meeting. It is essential to have constant emphasis about what people can do for themselves to change a situation. This doesn't happen in one meeting. Depending on relationships and trust, it can take many meetings and many months before an awareness of what can be accomplished begins to be established.

Once there is awareness raised and there seems to be interest in working toward a solution, the next step is asset assessment.

At every phase of the steps that follow, there should be one or two objectives in mind before approaching the step, so that the meeting or survey can be designed with the objective in mind and the leaders can look back to see if it was accomplished.

ASSET ASSESSMENT

An asset assessment is a great way to get people excited about what they have and what they can contribute to help solve a problem and change a situation that they've identified as important.

It helps to start with what people have rather than what they lack. This focuses on how to get people involved and excited about the process of investigation and problem solving. Individuals who live with less or in poverty may believe they have nothing to contribute. An asset assessment shows the opposite to be true. It points out the gifts God has given, natural talents, natural resources, strengths, and abilities that come from within individuals, churches, and communities that already exist. They are not dependent on outsiders. To get people to recognize they have possession of these "gifts," takes a facilitator familiar with the process and environment to makes it conducive for people to speak out without timidity.

Smaller groups are ideal. However the process can be done at a community meeting, with a church congregation, or in whatever setting would allow for free speech. One advantage of a larger group is that excitement can be built and is somewhat contagious. It can ignite an entire group to rally together for a cause.

Some questions that may be asked, once the group is comfortable together, are the following: (Assets should be listed as they are called out on a savable print material such as a white sheet, newsprint, etc. if available. If not, they should be put on a blackboard but someone should record the responses for future reference. It is important for the group to see the growing list of gifts and resources that they possess).

1. What gifts from God exist in this group (e.g., musicians, artists, cooks, hospitality, mechanical ability, technology expert, poetry, public-speaking, etc.)? Or in a restricted environment, what talents exist in this group (e.g., energy, passion, compassion, strength, joy, creativity, hard workers, etc.)?

2. What resources are present in this group (e.g., nurses, doctors, lawyers, young people, people connected to government, access to relatives at the bank, etc.)? Prompting questions may include: Does anyone have a garden, crops, cattle, goats, chickens, etc.?

3. What connections with other groups/agencies or policy makers exist within the group?

4. How can these resources be used to solve a community problem?

5. Does anyone have a story of how God used their gift or natural talent to help address a social need?

This process refers to "asset-based community development" (ABCD), a process developed by Cunningham and Mathie (as cited in Corbett & Fikkert, 2009). ABCD has four key elements critical to its successful process.

- It identifies, mobilizes, and builds on the skills and resources of the individuals in communities.

- It looks for resources and solutions to come from within the communities rather than from outside, whenever possible, relying on local and appropriate technology.

- It seeks to build relationships among various entities within the community such as church/community/social institutions, policy makers, etc., so that all community strengths are brought together.

- If outside resources are sought, this is done only when local initiative is not sufficient to meet the need and in a manner that will not create dependency and will allow for sustainability.

ASSET MAPPING

The next logical step in the process of working toward finding solutions in a participatory manner is to define a target area of involvement for outreach, and then to look at the physical layout and assets of that area. This is an interesting process of simply having groups of people sit down and draw a picture of their community and/or the area targeted. They are asked to identify the important structures and areas in that community, places where people meet, etc. Men, women, and youth will draw different maps as to what is important to them in the community. For example, the men may not even draw the market place, but the women will see it as a prominent part of their map. The youth may draw a place where the young people all hang out, but the adults may not put that place on their map. This serves as a guide to what resources exist in the community, where they are, and helps to guide people in thinking about how these institutions or meeting places can become leverage points or linkages to the problems that they wish to address. It may also be helpful in deciding where to begin a project or outreach and what some obstacles may be. For example, if everyone who does a map identifies a bad street where no one goes, then that becomes an important consideration. What makes it bad? Why can't people go there? Are there bad people there? What can be done? Obviously if an outreach to children is proposed, that street needs to be taken into account.

NEEDS ASSESSMENT

Only after generating insight and encouragement about what does exist right in the midst of the people themselves can one begin to take a look at what is needed. Starting with a needs assessment is often detrimental as it immediately sets up the idea of deficit. It may confirm the feeling, especially with those in poverty situations, that they are needy and need fixing. They view themselves as inferior and believe others come to save the day (Corbett & Fikkert, 2009).

A needs assessment is just that and can be done in similar fashion initially to the asset assessment explained above. Small groups can get together and discuss what the greatest need in the community is. There will not always be an agreement on this but it is an interesting challenge to discuss it. The activity outlined in the opening dialogue—i.e., having persons bring some article from home or the outside to represent what they feel is a need—gives people a little time to think about it and also provides a visual object to use to bring the issue home.

Needs assessment will usually take several forms, including the small group discussions, but will usually go beyond that to include some type of community survey. The survey is best when it is formulated by key persons from the church or community, as they will know what the right questions are, what will not be offensive culturally, and how to best get at the information that is needed. If the surveys will be done house-to-house, a decision by leaders will need to be made as to who would be the best people to conduct the survey. It would rarely ever be an outsider who would do this.

Decisions that need to be made include:

- What is the objective of the survey (e.g., to determine how many households in a given area are caring for a person who is terminally ill)?

- Who will compose the survey?

- What other information might be gleaned in the survey that will assist in the outreach? (e.g., how many people live in the home, is there medical help that comes to the home, etc.?)

- Who will conduct the survey, or how will the survey be conducted?

- Who will compile the results, or how will the results be compiled?

- What will be done with the information (i.e., who needs to be informed of the results, etc.)?

- How will the survey assist in formulating a plan of action?

Other ways of getting information are to tap into resources in the community such as the health department or local health facilities to see if they have already compiled statistics about the issues of the community and specifically about the questions being asked.

There are forms available that can be used to assess a community, from a simple, quick assessment to a very involved, detailed look at many different aspects of the community. These can be found online at <www.compassionlink.org>, under assessment tools.

WRITING OBJECTIVES

Probably the least favorite part of any outreach or project is that of writing the goals and objectives of what is to be accomplished. This, however, is one of the most important steps in the process, as it is on these objectives that everything else that follows will hinge. Even before doing the needs assessment, it is suggested that one or two objectives be formulated. This allows for designing the discussion or instrument to meet that objective and gives a way to look back to see if the objective has been accomplished.

Objectives serve a variety of purposes, but primarily they are created to help establish exactly what is to be accomplished by the outreach and to provide a way of measuring whether the intended outcome was achieved or not. Objectives answer the following questions:

1. *What* do you want to change?

2. For *whom* do you want the change to take place?

3. *How much* change do you want?

4. *Where* do you wish the change to take place?

5. *When* do you want the objective to be accomplished?

They should be written in such a way that they can meet the "SMART" criteria:

S : Specific
M : Measurable
A : Achievable
R : Relevant
T : Time-bound

Some examples of objectives are:

- Five workers will provide home care twice weekly for thirty people with AIDS in our community in the next year.

- To present the salvation message to twenty people and ask them to pray to receive Jesus during the home visits.

- To offer ten lessons on "Following Jesus" to those who pray to receive Jesus during the home visits in the next year.

PLAN OF ACTION

Once information is compiled and sorted out, a group of people can be appointed to draw up a Plan of Action. This is a great exercise to keep the outreach on target, to develop deadlines, and to give assignments. It is good to include as many people as possible from the original groups and to draw on the assets that were determined to exist among them.

A plan of action can be as simple or as involved as the members choose it to be. It can involve the outsiders as well as the local people, but it should not be dominated by the outsiders. Direction and guidance can be sought if needed, but care must be taken not to override local initiative because the ultimate goal is for the community/church to be mobilized into action in solving their own problem.

Community Mobilization, a term often used in development circles, simply means involving community members in the process of defining and transforming social problems. It builds a belief in its members that the community has knowledge and ability to get the job done and leaves people feeling good about what they have accomplished together. Part of this process involves mobilizing resources that already exist, disseminating information, generating support among each other, and fostering cooperation across public and private sectors in the community. It can be an ongoing process once it takes hold, and groups of people can begin to take on more and more responsibility for solving their own problems.

Recently a group in a rather remote area was called together for a community meeting. They'd been visited on occasion by outsiders and each time were given gifts and promised more to come in solving their issues. When asked how they might go about solving a particular community issue, one person replied to the visiting outsider, "Well, we just wait until you come and do it for us." Community mobilization, on the other hand, will work through the lengthy process of dialogue, asset assessment, and community mapping. This follows with needs assessment, plans of action, budgeting, and action implemented to solve the issue. This builds the people based on their amazing gifts, strengths, resources, and abilities they have to help guide and mobilize those capacities into action.

BUDGET PLANNING

Probably one of the more tedious and difficult steps in the process is projecting a budget for whatever the church/community decides to do. It is never possible to consider all the costs, but very necessary to attempt to put down everything that can possibly be considered.

A good budget also lists the most likely sources of income—offerings, donations from local donors, grants (which might be available locally), etc. Missionaries or outside entities may be able to declare what they can contribute to the budget at this time. A danger in this type of budget is in projecting salaries for individuals for ongoing work, especially not knowing at first if the project will survive.

At times, it becomes evident that the only way an outreach will manage to stay alive is with full-time, salaried persons in place. A carefully thought-through decision needs to be made at that time about whether there is a way to generate ongoing funds locally so that dependency on the outside donor doesn't mean the continued existence of the outreach. At the very least an exit strategy should be kept in focus for the donor funds in order for the outreach to be able to be sustained, should those outside funds not continue for some reason.

EVALUATION

An important part of the beginning steps of planning an outreach or intervention for a community issue is to determine the objectives as stated above. Once this is done, a plan for evaluating the results of the outreach can be put into place from the start. Ministries and missions circles often miss this step and make it more difficult to go back and look at results at a later time.

Evaluation is a subject too large to be covered in depth in this book. However, there are many fine texts and guides to doing evaluation in the contexts described in this book. One particular one that is easy to use and adapted for use in other country settings is *Looking Back, Looking Forward: A Participatory Guide to Evaluation by Heifer International* written by Asker and Shumaker (1994).

The important thing to remember is that an evaluation process is built on the objectives that are put forth, so they need to be measurable. Specific markers need to be identified so that the evaluators will know what kind of measures they will use to determine if the objective is being met. Important questions to answer before planning an evaluation are:

- Who will do the evaluation?

- How often will it be done?

- What will be done with the results?

There are also different outcomes that are being sought in an evaluation. It is one thing to look at "results" and another thing to look at "impact." One also wants to think of quality of the result and not just quantity. For example, everyone who came to the seminar said on the evaluation form that it was "very helpful information." The pre-test and post-test also showed that there was an increase in knowledge. So on two scores, the seminar might be evaluated successful. But did that helpful new information result in any change in behavior, method of doing things, attitudes, or the external problem? In other words, did the new information have any impact on the person that resulted in a change? Impact is an important consideration when thinking about and writing up objectives for an evaluation.

The main message of this text is that good stewardship demands evaluation! If all the above effort is done, the process itself is meaningful and good. But the only way to know if a change in a community—be it spiritual, physical, and/or emotional—has truly occurred, is to do an evaluation.

Once evaluation becomes a habit and the benefits of evaluation can be seen, it will not seem to be the daunting task that some envision it to be.

As mentioned earlier, George Bernard Shaw said, "The only man who behaves sensibly is my tailor; he takes my measurements anew every time he sees me, while all the rest go on with their old measurements and expect me to fit them."

THOUGHTS FOR CONSIDERATION

Appropriate technology is that which is designed with special consideration to the environmental, ethical, cultural, social, political, and economical aspects of the community for which it is intended. It typically requires fewer resources, is market-friendly, is easier to maintain, is more economically efficient, and has less of an impact on the environment compared to wasteful and environmentally polluting industrialized practices (Darrow & Saxenian, 1993).

Technology may be brought in and become so useful and practical to the local system that it is deemed "appropriate" because of its benefit. The mobile or cellular phone is a great example.

CHAPTER EIGHT

SUSTAINABLE SOLUTIONS

Monuments to poorly thought out solutions exist all over the world. Rusted images of plans gone awry—tractors, heavy machinery, combines, and more sit in the place where they breathed their last breath of life. They are a reminder to us of technology that didn't work. There were no funds for fuel, no spare parts available, no one with the ability to make repairs, and/or maybe just not the right equipment for that group of people or that project.

Buildings can also be a similar reminder and often an embarrassment to those who were involved in plans gone awry.

These would include multi-storied buildings that were intended to be hospitals, orphanages, community centers, or factories. The internal workings, however, were not figured into the budget or the plan of those who so enthusiastically constructed them. And so they sit, empty shells, often monuments to egos or to those who thought they knew best. They hadn't gone through the arduous and often time-consuming steps of figuring out what's happening and what needs to happen along with the people who know. No thought was given to local ownership and things arising "from the roots up."

I was once asked to assess a small clinic that had been constructed by a well-meaning group from the North. The group had come to work with a children's program in a particular country and decided that rather than have the children go to the many clinics that surrounded the church/school compound, it would be best to have a clinic right there, immediately accessible for the children, teachers, and church members and workers. It was felt that it could also be opened up to the families of the children, thereby becoming a drawing point to get families into the area. It was hoped that it would be a witness to them of the love and care of the church.

The building, consisting of many small rooms and a small waiting area, was constructed by a small team of builders who came from a church in the US. As I did the assessment of the building itself, it was immediately clear, first, that a medical person had not been consulted when the plans had been made. The way in which the clinic was laid out made traffic flow and passing from one service to the next an almost impossible task.

It limited the number of people that could be in the halls or building at one time.

Second, the need for the clinic was not thought through. A quick assessment of the local community surrounding the church compound turned up five small clinics all within easy walking distance and all able to offer the same type of service this clinic was intended to offer.

Third, it had never really been established who would pay the salaries of the medical personnel who worked at the clinic, how medications and supplies would be procured, and unless market prices were charged, how the little clinic would be sustained.

Lastly, security issues for the church compound would increase tenfold by having medications on the property. A security guard would have to be employed, and a wall would need to be constructed around the church. No one was certain how funds would be secured.

In the final analysis, during multiple meetings with the church leaders and others, it became clear that though all thought it would be a nice service to offer and have available, it was really not something with enough priority for the church and its members. They were not willing to invest their own funds. When a realistic budget was drawn up, they realized that the prices that would have to be charged for the care and medications would be the same as or higher than they were already paying.

Sustainability has become somewhat of a buzzword in many circles today, but for the purpose of transformational development, it remains a very important concept. When sustainability becomes part of the equation of considering solutions to problems, there is more likelihood for an ongoing, long-term effectiveness to whatever is undertaken.

DEFINING SUSTAINABILITY

Sustainability is defined as the ability of an entity to fulfill its mission effectively and consistently over time by developing, procuring and managing sufficient resources (human capacities, giftings, finances, etc.) without creating dependency on external sources. It is obvious from this definition that sustainability is about more than just finances. The entire spectrum of human experience needs to be considered in whatever is undertaken, human resources, spiritual impact, emotional outlay, as well as finances. Can, for example, volunteerism be sustained over the life of the outreach? Will those same volunteers be able to withstand the tragedy of seeing persons die from AIDS if home care ministry is a goal? The life and ongoing impact of a project can be threatened by the inability to sustain any part of the outreach by the people who are involved.

Sustainability also refers to the ability of the impact of whatever is undertaken to continue on into the future. That may or may not be a goal, but certainly at least some of the aspects of the outreach will want to be able to be sustained over time. Is that possible, and if not, should the outreach be undertaken at all or scaled back to a manageable proportion so that sustainability might be achieved?

It should be noted that, though financial sustainability and lack of dependence on outside funding is a goal, there is also a recognition that local financial capacity may never rise to be able to meet the need that is to be addressed. This needs to be acknowledged and the life of the outreach planned and accepted in that light.

MISSIONARY-DRIVEN PROJECTS & SUSTAINABILITY

Reference has been made in earlier chapters to the missionary who arrives on the field ready to put his or her burden or call into action. Often, without going through the rigors of the dialogue and assessment process, or by deciding that the local church is not interested, the missionary decides to launch his or her ministry without the local church. Church leadership may have given a nod of approval to allow the missionary to do the ministry. Unfortunately, there was little or no attempt by the missionary to work in, through, and with the local group of believers or with a targeted group of community members in the case where a church did not yet exist.

After some time, when the ministry flourishes, and is subsidized or paid in full by mission funds, it is time for the missionary to go home, change fields, or move on to other things. This can be when the handover occurs. The ministry is handed off or given over to the church to continue. I've often heard it said, "I got it started and then gave it to them." We wonder why in fact that ministry isn't flourishing quite so well in the hands of the nationals. I've also heard, "They just can't do quite as well." And I sigh, wondering why they should be able to do as well when they've not had any ownership in the ministry. They weren't involved in its formation, probably didn't really want it to be handed over, may not have been trained for its function, and are struggling to figure out how to fund it now that it is theirs to operate.

It is so much better to start together. If there doesn't seem to be a vision or burden in the hearts of the local church people for a particular ministry, perhaps over time, as relationships are built and opportunities arise, vision for that particular outreach can be cast. But meanwhile, if the dialogue and assessment process are put in motion with the same group, they could identify the issues that are on their hearts. They could articulate their vision for the issues they would like to address, and perhaps the missionary could put his or her agenda aside to work with what the church feels is priority.

When the Lord births a vision, He has a way of eventually bringing it into focus. However, the timing may not be that of our own choosing nor in the way that we originally thought it would happen. Working beside the local church people and validating their concerns and issues would put the missionary so far down the road in relationship building and cultural understanding and gaining the friends in mission and ministry that were referred to in chapter seven.

APPROPRIATE TECHNOLOGY

It isn't possible to discuss sustainability without discussing appropriate technology, as well. The way in which technology is changing the way of life of so many in the developing world today is outstanding. Technology is opening up the world to those who have rarely had a glimpse, and it has, for the most part, an amazing and positive role to play in the development arena. But for all the advances of technology in recent years, it is still important to use the word *appropriate* when referring to it.

Appropriate technology is that which is designed with special consideration to the environmental, ethical, cultural, social, political, and economical aspects of the community for which it is intended (Darrow & Saxenian, 1993). It typically requires fewer resources, is market-friendly, is easier to maintain, more economically efficient, and has less of an impact on the environment compared to wasteful and environmentally polluting industrialized practices. According to Darrow & Saxenian (1993) the following criteria are necessary for a product to be considered an appropriate technology (AT):

- requires only small amounts of capital;

- emphasizes the use of locally available materials, in order to lower costs and reduce supply problems;

- is relatively labor-intensive but more productive than many traditional technologies;

- is small enough in scale to be affordable to individual families or small groups of families;

- can be understood, controlled, and maintained by villagers whenever possible, without a high level of specific training;

- can be produced in villages or small workshops;

- supposes that people can and will work together to bring improvements to communities;

- offers opportunities for local people to become involved in the modification and innovation process;

- is flexible, and can be adapted to different places and changing circumstances;

- can be used in productive ways without doing harm to the environment.

Some examples of appropriate technology would be a decision to use solar cookers for fuel conservation in a certain community. An assessment has revealed that there are fewer and fewer trees, women have to walk many miles and carry heavy loads and often spend the majority of their day trying to find fuel. If illness strikes, there is no way to get fuel and consequently no way to cook food. There is not enough money to purchase charcoal or wood.

A good, solid solar cooker can be imported from another country for about eighty US dollars each, or a cardboard foil-covered solar shield can be constructed in the village using local materials for about five dollars each. Though the local product will not be as durable and will not cook as well, it is a much more feasible solution to begin to address the problem. A long-range goal may be that of figuring out a construction model that could be made locally that would be a better product, last longer, and cook better.

Another example is that of water purification. If unclean water and the consequences of that has been identified as a priority problem through the assessment process and there is consensus that getting clean water in the area is a priority, then a decision about appropriate technology comes into play.

As in the example of the tractors and equipment that lie dormant, are equal examples of water wells with pumps that no longer work, and cement tops over wells that have been smashed so that buckets could be put down because the pump ceased to work. Parts to fix it were not available and it was therefore no longer useful.

Ownership of whatever method of water purification is decided upon is so important. The method of purifying and getting the water needs to be owned by the people who will use it, as well. Well-digging has become a popular *intervention* from the outside, but often goes awry because the dialogue, assessment, and ownership process was not gone through and input of those who will use the water was not sought. A well was simply dug for people. It was probably appreciated as long as it lasted, but it was not owned by the people who use it.

If a well is to be the best solution, how can everyone in the community be involved in the entire process of obtaining the well? How can the well be owned by all? If it's a filtration system, can all of the system be built and maintained by using local resources? If a system or some of its parts need to be imported from the outside, it probably won't be as easy to repair and maintain. If ownership of the clean water is spread throughout the community, it allows the people, whose children do better because of less diarrhea, feel good about being part of that solution.

Appropriate technology does not exclude technology that comes from elsewhere. Technology may be brought in and become so useful and practical to the local system that it is deemed appropriate because of its benefit. The mobile or cellular phone is a great example. This is a product that is literally changing the lives of thousands of people across the world.

Cell phones not only offer opportunities through voice services, but due to emerging technologies that bring Internet access to phones, people now have connections to services—and literally to the world—that are life-changing and nullify the need of an expensive computer. For example, once phones were rare in much of Tanzania due to poor wire-line infrastructure, but a recent study found 97 percent of people said they could access a mobile phone, while only 28 percent could access a landline.

Research in India and Africa has found Internet connectivity can be key to improving the livelihood of rural poor by giving them access to information—everything from crop prices to the legal protocol to acquiring tenure to land. Internet access can simplify interaction with government institutions for mundane tasks like acquiring an identity card as well as potentially increasing transparency and reducing corruption in transactions with officials. Persons can pay bills, transfer money, and even make payments on their microcredit right from their cell phones. Also, because calling plans are often pre-paid, there is no need for a bank account or credit check. Entire books can now be uploaded to cellular phones for a minimal fee thus providing opportunities that might never have been possible without the availability of this technology (Denison, n.d.).

I recently heard of a clinic who calls its patients on cell phones to remind them to take their pills. This replaced the need for the patient to go to the clinic on a daily basis. In the past, this was the normal way that long-term, complicated medications were given.

Computers and Internet access, though often not affordable for the average person, can be accessed in internet cafes and online stations. I made a visit back to the DRC not too long ago and was amazed to find, not only cell phones (still no electricity—but charging by solar power), but Internet stations around the town. In my day of residence there, one had to travel by air all the way across the country to make a phone call.

ECONOMIC DEVELOPMENT

The term *economic development* can refer to many different arenas in sustainable development and is too large a topic to cover completely in this book. However, it is gaining in popularity in providing means by which outside entities can be involved in assistance through various levels of micro-finance, micro-loans, and the now popular, business as missions, which itself has many meanings.

Globalization has brought many changes to the developing world and has impacted poverty in both positive and negative ways. It refers to the shrinking or removal of barriers between national borders in order to facilitate the flow of goods, capital, services, and labor. There are many advantages to globalization as the borders open up. Some of the advantages are:

- Increase in trade opportunities

- Increased awareness of the world

- Technology more available to the poor

- Able to get goods in faster—especially in disaster situations

- The Gospel reaches more people

But for billions of the world's people, business-driven globalization means uprooting old ways of life and threatening livelihoods and cultures. The disadvantages particularly to those living with less are:

- Markets can fail causing economic decline

- Trafficking, drug running, and weapons more easily accessible across borders

- Imports all that is bad from other places

- Can reduce jobs/markets

- Traditional ways of small business marketing and selling can be overrun with the new technology

- Immigration can bring a preponderance of a religion that was minimally present in a culture before, such as the great influx of Islam into Europe. (Of course, this can be an advantage if it's bringing Christ to a non-Christian area.)

Globalization, then, has helped to shape the method and means of economic development. Many new techniques are learned and imported simply by the availability of information from such sources as the Internet. Many business entrepreneurs from one land will find their way to another to begin businesses, which in some instances, will be of benefit to the culture where it is found, and in other instances, will have no intention of being of benefit, but is there only to make a profit.

So, what is the role of the missionary or church member from another land when it comes to economic development? Is it an arena of help that can be offered and does it fit in the transformational development model?

DEFINING ECONOMIC DEVELOPMENT

For the missionary and local church, economic development, like and as a part of transformational development, has a goal of building the capacity of people to be able to help and support themselves and their families. In the process, the goal is for the people to be reconciled to Jesus and to find His will and plan for their lives.

As stated earlier, economic development can take many forms, but in this book, the following will be considered; micro-finance (also referred to as micro-enterprise, micro-loans, and micro-banking) and business as mission.

MICROFINANCE

The well-known Bangladesh professor and Nobel Peace Prize winner of 2006, Dr. Muhammad Yunus, has made micro-finance known to much of the world. It is being used globally to provide economic empowerment to many in the developing world (Corbett & Fikkert, 2009). Dr. Yunus developed a bank or banking system, called the Grameen Bank, which offers Grameen credit. The following information is taken from the Grameen Bank (2009) website:

General features of Grameen credit are:

- It promotes credit as a human right.

- Its mission is to help the poor families help themselves to overcome poverty. It is targeted to the poor, particularly poor women.

- The most distinctive feature of Grameen credit is that it is not based on any collateral, or legally enforceable contracts. It is based on trust, not on legal procedures and system.

- It is offered for creating self-employment for income-generating activities and housing for the poor, as opposed to consumption.

- It was initiated as a challenge to the conventional banking, which rejected the poor by classifying them to be not creditworthy. As a result, it rejected the basic methodology of the conventional banking and created its own methodology.

- It provides service at the doorstep of the poor based on the principle that the people should not go to the bank, banking should go to the people.

- In order to obtain loans, a borrower must join a group of borrowers.

- Loans can be received in a continuous sequence. New loans become available to a borrower if her previous loan is repaid.

- All loans are to be paid back in installments (weekly, or bi-weekly).

- Simultaneously more than one loan can be received by a borrower.

- It comes with both obligatory and voluntary savings programs for the borrowers.

- Generally these loans are given through non-profit organizations or through institutions owned primarily by the borrowers. If it is done through for-profit institutions not owned by the borrowers, efforts are made to keep the interest rate at a level which is close to a level commensurate with sustainability of the program rather than bringing an attractive return for the investors. Grameen credit's thumb-rule is to keep the interest rate as close to the prevailing market rate, prevailing in the commercial banking sector as possible, without sacrificing sustainability. In fixing the interest rate market interest rate is taken as the reference rate, rather than the moneylender's rate. Reaching the poor is its non-negotiable mission. Reaching sustainability is a directional goal. It must reach sustainability as soon as possible, so that it can expand its outreach without fund constraints.

- Grameen credit gives high priority on building social capital. It is promoted through formation of groups and centers, developing leadership quality through annual election of group and center leaders, and electing board members when the institution is owned by the borrowers. To develop a social agenda owned by the borrowers, something similar to the *sixteen decisions*, it undertakes a process of intensive discussion among the borrowers, and encourages them to take these decisions seriously and implement them. It gives special emphasis on the formation of human capital and concern for protecting environment. It monitors children's education, provides scholarships and student loans for higher education. For formation of human capital it makes efforts to bring technology, like mobile phones, solar power, and promote mechanical power to replace manual power.

Grameen credit is based on the premise that the poor have skills which remain unutilized or underutilized. It is definitely not the lack of skills which make poor people poor. Grameen believes that the poverty is not created by the poor. It is created by the institutions and policies which surround them. In order to eliminate poverty, all we need to do is to make appropriate changes in the institutions and policies, and/or create new ones. Grameen believes that charity is not an answer to poverty. It only helps poverty to continue. It creates dependency and takes away an individual's initiative to break through the wall of poverty. Unleashing of energy and creativity in each human being is the answer to poverty.

Grameen brought credit to the poor, women, the illiterate, and the people who pleaded that they did not know how to invest money and earn an income. Grameen created a methodology and an institution around the financial needs of the poor, and created access to credit on reasonable terms, enabling the poor to build on their existing skills to earn a better income in each cycle of loans. (Grameen Bank web site, December 2009).

> The life story of Ammajan Amina, one of Grameen's first borrowers, illustrates what micro-credit can do for a street beggar. Of her six children, four had died of hunger or disease. Only two daughters survived. Her husband, who was much older than she, was ill. For several years he had spent most of the family assets trying to find a cure.
>
> After his death, all that Amina had left was the house. She was in her forties, which is old by Bangladesh standards,

she was illiterate and she had never earned an income before. Her in-laws tried to expel her and her children from the house where she had lived for 20 years, but she refused to leave.

She tried selling homemade cakes and biscuits door-to-door, but one day she returned to find her brother-in-law had sold her tin roof and the buyer was busy removing it. Now the rainy season started and she was cold, hungry and too poor to make food to sell. All she had she used to feed her own children.

Because she was a proud woman, she begged but only in nearby villages. As she had no roof to protect her house, the monsoon destroyed her mud walls. One day when she returned, she found her house had collapsed and she started screaming: "Where is my daughter? Where is my baby?" She found her older child, dead under the rubble of her house.

When Professor Yunus's colleague Nurjahan met her in 1976, she held her only surviving child in her arms. She was hungry, heartbroken and desperate. There was no question of any money lender, much less a commercial bank, giving her credit, but with small loans she started making bamboo baskets and remained a borrower to the end of her days. Now her daughter is a member of Grameen. (Grameen Bank web site, 2009).

It seems a simple concept, yet there are multiple issues to consider when beginning such a program. Though it seems like a wonderful way to give assistance, it can also cause resentment and frustration if proper attention is not given to the details of who actually owns the loan business, who collects the loans, who holds the borrower accountable, who sets the interest rates, and most importantly, who decides who gets the money if there isn't enough for everyone who is seeking a loan.

There is also some thought that microloans and micro business in some slums, particularly in patriarchal societies may not work well. The reasons for this are many but include the concept that though women are often the recipients of the loans and the ones to set up the small business, the earnings would by virtue of culture be turned over to the men. Also, because of the high volume of loans that could be given in a confined area for the same or similar type of small business, competition would be high making profit difficult. There is also the issue in African culture that a "business owner" regardless of the size of the business may have an obligation to provide for the extended family, so that any profit made would need to be shared with the many who would come to claim their rights as "family" (Karnani, 2007). Karnani (2007) suggests that a better alternative, is some cultures that deal with some of the issues that were just outlined, would benefit more from the creation of a macro enterprise, where jobs were provided. In this way, women could go and work for a wage and a product that was proven to be needed and usable by that particular market could be manufactured more efficiently and sold less expensively. The family pressure, it is felt, would not be as great for a wage earner as for a business owner. Each culture and market situation would need to be carefully assessed and each community engaged in repeated dialogue before these types of activities would be considered.

On the other hand, most poor people have no access to banks and are often at the mercy of loan sharks who exact huge interest rates and payments just for handling the money of their borrowers.

Corbett & Fikkert (2009) contend that missionaries and churches make very poor business providers and should think seriously before taking on a microfinance initiative. They feel that these two groups are particularly ill-suited to take on this challenge because they traditionally lack the technical, managerial, and business acumen to make the program financially sustainable. Another reason, these authors feel it ill-advised for churches and missionaries to be involved, is their particular culture of grace. They would be hard-pressed to be the ones with the discipline needed to enforce the repayment of loans.

Some groups have successfully managed the above issues by forming an entity that is church-related but is not the church itself. They have comprised a board or committee often of church members who do possess the necessary business skills to put together a business plan. Along with the loans, there is usually training on stewardship and simple business principles. Often there is teaching on tithing and giving back to the Lord, as well.

Women are the more common recipients of loans and have been shown to be the most likely to repay them. Many organizations provide a payback incentive by not charging interest for the first year. Some institutions report 90 percent or more in payback figures (Grameen Bank web site, 2009).

CHURCH-BASED SAVINGS & CREDIT ASSOCIATIONS

A model which is gaining popularity—and which does not require any outside funding—is that of savings and credit associations that are a part of the church and/or exist alongside the church. In this model, each member of the association contributes a set amount to the fund of their own savings or money they have earned. The members of the association decide how much will be lent, to whom it will be lent and the terms of the loan. At a predetermined time, each member's money is returned to them along with the dividends they've earned from the interest charged on the loans. Then everyone decides if they wish to reinvest and the cycle begins again. The advantage of this system is that it doesn't require outside funds and that it is truly owner-based and owner-run. It can also give out very small loans, which is something that the larger programs cannot always do.

The disadvantages are that people are not always good at managing the program, deciding who should receive the benefit, and they often become impatient with the process. Overall, though, there is merit to this type of system, especially in small, rural communities.

The role of missionaries and/or the church is simply to help to facilitate the formation of such a program and to offer advice or counsel as requested.

BUSINESS AS MISSION

Another economic development method that has gained in popularity among the donor population is that of business as mission. This again has taken many forms, but basically the concept is to begin a for-profit business that will help to alleviate poverty in a variety of ways. This alleviation may be in the form of employment of persons in the business or by making money from the business which can be infused into the poverty situation in some way. The business may provide funds for the micro-credit bank to make loans.

Business as mission provides opportunities for Christian businesspersons to become involved in missions. They can use their expertise in training in business principles, planning, marketing, record keeping, etc., and helping those in other countries begin their own small businesses. Businesspersons are excellent resources for churches or groups who are interested in starting some type of income generating project or microcredit program from or alongside their church.

The needs of the world grow ever more urgent. HIV/AIDS, malaria, and other diseases take away the productive energy of entire groups of people. Droughts and famines undermine even the most sincere efforts to make life work. It seems appropriate in these unprecedented days of need to look for every way and means for people to help themselves. Sometimes just a small loan will make all the difference in whether lives continue in misery and abject poverty or whether, with that small loan, there is hope to break out of the drudgery and make something new happen.

When the love of Jesus can be seen and shared in the mix of economic development, the transformational process takes on new meaning. Often principles of tithing, stewardship, saving, and prudent spending, as well as solid biblical principles are taught in loan classes along with principles of financial management. Testimonies begin to give glory to God, not solely to the loan institution that gave the money.

THOUGHTS FOR CONSIDERATION

We must be willing to lay aside our time consciousness and our need for immediate gratification in deference to the process of time that may be required for true change to take place.

We truly need to honor the dignity and worth of those we desire to work alongside and realize that no matter their plight in life, they have giftings and talents and resources to bring to the table.

EMBRACING CHANGE

Whenever I speak on change, I always ask how many like change. Usually there are a few who tell me that they do. They enjoy the challenge of change, and I imagine at some level, most people would agree that, without any change at all, life would truly become dull.

However, change from the way it has always been done to embracing new paradigms and new ways of thinking entails a process, one that can be uncomfortable. Occasionally "Aha!" moments occur along the way, but for most, change evolves over time as new ideas are introduced in different ways. These are usually reinforced by respected individuals and groups in a variety of settings.

In my own mission, compassion ministries have not always been highly regarded, though almost always done. In the early days, there was a concern that by becoming involved in caring for social needs, the mandate of witnessing and evangelism of the lost and discipling the found would be diluted.

The era of the social gospel gave momentum to that line of thinking. Social gospel proponents felt that simply doing good works was sufficient without the necessity of proclaiming a message of repentance and salvation. There were also some denominations that were involved in large institutions such as hospitals and schools abroad. Though their original intent had been to incorporate a spiritual component, that had gotten lost in government requirements or simply the business of running an institution. Many times there were restrictions on hiring only Christians and these institutions became money-drainers with very little tangible evangelistic thrust.

My Pentecostal denomination, as well as others, has a strong emphasis on divine healing. Therefore, a focus on medical outreach and institutions, when some of our leaders were opposed or suspicious of the medical world, brought dissonance in the ranks. My own father was a divine healing evangelist who did not believe in going to a physician. Thus the leaders of my own movement, in earlier times, were strong in their urging to avoid the distractions of social work and to stay on the task of evangelizing as many as possible.

When our mission finally did become intentional about sending missionaries to do compassion ministries assignments, there was still much disagreement about what priority that should receive. There was also uncertainty as to how it should be documented and recorded as part of our missiology. And we were divided in our views of what constituted holistic ministry. I recall a meeting where almost an entire day was spent by some fifty people debating whether the word *holistic* could even be used in our context. Ultimately, it was decided that it had too much baggage and should not be used, and they chose the phrase "ministry to the whole person." The same discussion occurred regarding the term *humanitarian*, and it was also not chosen as a term to be used in our documentation. These discussions were being held in the late 1990s, not that long ago.

It is not surprising, then, that entering late into intentional ministries of compassion, there continues to be a paucity of education and knowledge when it comes to foundational principles of what constitutes "best practice" in this arena. Many practitioners find themselves doing what has been done before, what they inherit from someone else, or what seems to be the most practical thing to do with the need that is presented.

Over the years my mission, recognizing this, has taken steps to begin to bring compassion practitioners together annually and to present principles of sound missiological practice, and over time, this will begin to make a difference.

PARADIGM SHIFTS

Paradigms shift and change. It has happened in my mission. It happens in medicine. Actually, it happens in almost every aspect of our lives. The way things were often done isn't the way things are now. Steven Covey (2004) in his well-known book, *Seven Habits of Highly Effective People,* includes an illustration that points out how our paradigm changes when we have different information. Covey was traveling in a subway when a man got in with his two sons. The boys were running all over the place bothering people, and as this continued, he got irritated enough to ask the father why he didn't do something to control his kids. The father replied, "We just got back from the hospital where their mother died. I don't know how to handle it and I guess they don't either."

Suddenly you see everything differently. That is the power of a paradigm shift. They are the same kids yelling and screaming in the subway, but you look at them and understand them in a different way.

It has also happened in compassion ministries practice. What was once considered good or best practice ten or twenty years ago, may now, due to research or similar experience of many, simply is not considered to be good or best. Yet that information takes time to be disseminated.

In the early days of paternalistic missions where things were done for instead of with the people and churches on the field, those missionaries that did feel a compulsion to be involved in compassion ministries often tried to provide clothing and cover up for those without clothes. The missionaries would respond to needs that they saw by trying to provide medical care, dentistry (often in the backyard with a pair of pliers), or taking in orphans because there seemed no other alternative. Because it was the paradigm of "doing for," the label of "great white father" or "mother" or "provider" was often given as the missionaries tried (though often in vain) to meet the needs around them.

A paradigm shift came ushering in the era of partnership and a move away from the doing *for* and toward a more indigenous doing *with*. For those missionaries just moving into that era, it was for some a very painful time, as the expectation of the people that they came to serve was that the outsider was to provide. When provisions weren't forthcoming, it was often seen as a lack of love or an unwillingness to share what they had, and it caused some missionaries to become bitter and disappointed in their experience. It also caused some nationals to begin to mistrust the system. A lot of misunderstandings occurred as this shift had not been properly prepared for or explained in some areas.

Paradigm shifts are at times imperceptible, but more often for those in the midst of the change, they are not without some pain and struggle.

I recall some dear friends who got caught in just such a time. They had built a beautiful children's home with help from churches in the US. It had state-of-the-art dorms, teaching facilities, playgrounds, kitchen, and recreation areas and seemed like it should be a perfect place for children to be housed after being rescued from the streets. A lot of time, energy, and money went into its construction. But its completion occurred about the time that people were beginning to talk about the negative aspects of institutions and different ways to care for orphaned and abandoned children. It became a very painful struggle between co-workers, missionaries, and nationals, and ultimately resulted in the loss of the missionaries from the field. No one could really be blamed in that situation. It was just poor timing more than anything.

There has also been a paradigm shift in the way that governments view certain social outreaches, including the care of children. "Community based" is a paradigm shift now that is an important consideration to any project that hopes to be awarded funding from an agency that has any government links. The feeling is that communities should care for their own. They should be responsible for persons with HIV/AIDS or for orphans. Therefore, children's care or hospice care or home care of any kind needs to be in and of and by the community that it represents if it is to be funded.

Another associate of mine, not knowing that the paradigm shift to community-based care had occurred, felt he was doing the right thing by building group homes instead of orphanages for the many children orphaned by HIV/AIDS in his country. He has homes of simple construction, house parents from the country so that the children would be raised according to local custom and culture, and all seemed well except that the homes were outside of town on a farm and the children were removed from their own communities to go to these homes. Unfortunately for him, none of the large funding agencies would give him any funds because his project was not community based. A shift that fifteen years before would not have been an issue, is now considered to be of utmost importance to the funding agencies.

Most of us working in compassion ministries have changed our methodologies over the years as new information and experience has become available. Myers (1999) says it well when speaking of the journey toward transformational development, and he reminds us that human progress is not inevitable; it takes hard work...Everyone is on the journey: the poor, the non-poor, and the staff of the development agency.

The givers and receivers of assistance and the donors may all be at different points in their journey of knowledge and experience of the "shift" of the paradigm or have no knowledge of it at all. This can and does at times become the cause of dissonance between partners because the parties are not even aware that they are at different points on the paradigm continuum.

GENERATIONAL SHIFTS

Interestingly, there are paradigm shifts that come about as generations pass from one to another. We go from the Boomers to the genXers to the Millennials or the Y generation, all of whom seem to be with us at the time of this writing.

As we move from one group to the next, there seems to be more and more movement toward hands-on involvement with social cause and humanitarian concerns. I am so impressed with the young people that I meet who have already started their own non-profit organizations and are ready to go and make a difference somewhere in the world. And, as I said in the preface of this book, I remain just a little concerned about what they may not know.

Yet, their hearts and passion are so right. Those who love the Lord want to put that love and compassion into action that truly makes a difference. The challenge for us, who have been down the road and on the journey for a while, is how to channel their love, compassion, and enthusiasm. We also need to find how to provide bits and pieces of foundational information that won't stifle or slow down their enthusiasm, but will build upon it with knowledge that I know will make sense to them once heard.

What I see in these young people is a keen sense of wanting to do what is right. I observe a wonderful sense of respect for the dignity of others and a much greater sense of equality and lack of discrimination that my generation may have possessed, due to our socialization.

I believe the future is bright for missions, for the world in need, and for the ability for partnerships and true friendships to occur between the *haves* and *have nots*. I believe that with borders shrinking and technology bringing us closer and closer, we can have missions coming from everywhere, going to everywhere. I believe we will do it using every available means and that the tangible demonstrations of compassion are part of the Good News of the Kingdom of God.

RESPONSES, PARADIGM SHIFTS, & NEW INFORMATION

To some readers, this is new information. Others will have heard this before and this text will hopefully serve as a reinforcement of seeds that have already been planted on the journey to change.

For some, these thoughts will actually generate excitement as they may serve to motivate and provide foundation for plans that are already in motion or at least in the dreaming stages. Whatever your case may be, I implore you to at least give thought to what has been stated in the preceding chapters.

There is so much that needs to be accomplished, and so much that can be accomplished by persons of like faith who truly want to see the world won to Jesus and the needs of the world diminished. There are huge injustices that need to be addressed and the voice of the members of the body of Christ needs to be heard. The action of the Church needs to reverberate throughout communities and societies and nations. We all, working together can, and should, be involved in integrated ministry and mission. As we understand these principles of Kingdom work, we can and will make a difference for now and eternity. But ...

- Egos must be set aside.

- There is no time or room for personal agendas that override the building of relationships.

- The "feel good benevolence" that may have been a driving force in the past, must give way to the development of those we are sent to serve.

- We must be willing to lay aside our time consciousness and our need for immediate gratification in deference to the process of time that may be required for true change to take place.

- We truly need to honor the dignity and worth of those we desire to work alongside and realize that no matter their plight in life, they have giftings and talents and resources to bring to any life equation.

- We cannot override others giftings in our need to accomplish and provide and rescue and be the "god" in their lives. We must give them time and opportunity to help themselves and to be all that God intended them to be.

I urge us all to earnestly pray and search our hearts and examine our motives and the forces that drive us *to go* and *to give* and *build* and *take care of.* All of these things are good. But they may not be best.

Let us commit ourselves to want the best for those we serve.

Let us commit ourselves to study, to research, to ask questions, and to really know the people we serve.

Let us commit to friendships first, letting money, projects, buildings and programs be secondary to relationships.

Then let us trust each other enough to work for the common good, going at a pace that seems right to both friends.

And lastly, let us always ask ourselves how it would be in reverse. What if I were in need and someone was coming from another place to help me? What would I want? How would I wish to be approached? What would my priority needs be?

Let us be prayerful, wise, and cautious, yet never let our hands or hearts be closed. There are so many viable ways that we can partner together to make meaningful contributions.

David Sanford (2008) has paraphrased 1 Corinthians 13 from the social perspective.

> If I talk a lot about God and the Bible and the Church, but I fail to ask about your needs and then help you, I'm simply making a lot of empty religious noise.

> If I graduate from theological seminary and know all the answers to questions you'll never even think of asking, and if I have all the degrees to prove it and if I say I believe in God with all my heart, and soul and strength, and claim to have incredible answers to my prayers to show it, but I fail to take the time to find out where you're at and what makes you laugh and why you cry, I'm nothing.

> If I sell an extra car and some of my books to raise money for some poor starving kids somewhere, and if I give my life for God's service and burn out after pouring everything I have into the work, but do it all without ever once thinking about the people, the real hurting people—the moms and dads and sons and daughters and orphans and widows and the lonely and hurting—if I pour my life into the Kingdom but forget to make it relevant to those here on earth, my energy is wasted, and so is my life.

Helpful Web Sites

APPROPRIATE TECHNOLOGY

Appropriate Technology Africa

Appropriate Technology Africa provides technology to empower poor people in Africa to make sellable end-user products. Concentrating specifically on the African market, Appropriate Technology Africa has come up with appropriate, relevant, reliable and cost-effective solutions to meet small business needs. ATA does this without compromising on quality.

<http://www.approtechafrica.com>

Appropriate Technology Collaborative

The Appropriate Technology Collaborative is a not-for-profit organization whose purpose is to design, develop, demonstrate and distribute appropriate technological solutions for meeting the basic human needs of low income people in the developing world. ATC works in collaboration with clients and other nonprofits and NGOs to create technologies that are culturally sensitive, environmentally responsible and locally repairable in order to improve the quality of life, enhance safety, and reduce adverse impacts on their environment.

<http://apptechdesign.org>

Centre for Appropriate Technology

The Centre for Appropriate Technology works to secure sustainable livelihoods for communities of indigenous people through appropriate technology. CAT provides information, knowledge and practical services across a range of areas including energy, housing and infrastructure, water, waste, telecommunications, transport and technical skills development. CAT utilizes evidence-based and applied problem solving approaches to assist communities of Indigenous people to access the information, services and skills required to live safe and happy lives.

<http://www.icat.org.au>

Engineers Without Borders

Engineers Without Borders is an international humanitarian engineering group that serves global neighbors in the developing world; those who need it most. They provide the basics of life such as water and shelter, using appropriate and sustainable technology. More importantly, they help people help themselves. Their unique model includes a rigorous technical and cultural assessment, community involvement, and a five-year commitment to each community they are privileged to serve. Dedicated professionals and aspiring college students form the backbone of EWB, with invaluable help from corporations, non-government organizations, and other supporters.

<http://www.ewb-usa.org>

Global Village Institute for Appropriate Technology

Global Village is a non-profit organization created for the purpose of researching promising new technologies that can benefit humanity in environmentally friendly ways. The philosophy of the Institute is that emerging technologies that link the world together are not ethically neutral, but often have long-term implications for viability of natural systems, human rights and our common future. The site has many helpful articles on multiple facets of technology, including solar devices, mechanical devices, water systems, animal husbandry, agriculture, and many more.

<http://www.thefarm.org/charities/i4at/library.html>

International Development Enterprise

IDE is a unique international non-profit organization that has been helping poor farmers in developing countries escape poverty for more than 25 years. IDE has pioneered a market-based approach that has enabled millions to permanently escape poverty. IDE uses business principles to facilitate unsubsidized market systems in which the rural poor can effectively participate as micro-entrepreneurs and earn income. In this way, their programs create an environment that helps small farmers progress from subsistence agriculture to commercial farming, beginning an upward spiral out of chronic deprivation and vulnerability.

<http://www.ideorg.org>

Sustain Hope

Sustain Hope is an international ministry of the Assemblies of God World Missions that is focused on community development using appropriate technology. The team of missionaries is available to assist with participatory assessment, community dialogue and planning, market analysis and help with determining sustainable solutions. They prefer to work with and through local churches when possible.

<http://www.sustainhope.org>

CHILDREN

Bible-Centered Ministries International

The 4-14 Window is defined as that window of opportunity between the ages of four to fourteen when more than 85 percent of Christians make their decision to follow Christ. With more than 2 billion children falling into this category and almost half the world's population under 21, BCM International has made this strategic 4-14 Window the central focus of its ministry since beginning as the Bible Club Movement in 1936. All around the world BCM is committed to partnering with local churches to reach children for Christ and disciple them in God's Word.

<http://bcmintl.org>

Bible Visuals International

BVI publications are being used in over 150 countries by missionaries and nationals in over 70 mission agencies. Translations of BVI materials are available in over 80 languages. In addition to the 78-volume Visualized Bible Series, BVI products include child-appealing visualized stories, visualized hymns of the faith, clip art and the Give-A-Vision Programs for teaching missions to children.

<http://www.biblevisuals.org>

Convoy of Hope

Convoy of Hope desires to minister to meet the food needs of children worldwide by means of community outreaches, responding to disasters, developing healthy communities and assuring the sustainability of ongoing food security.

<http://www.convoyofhope.org>

Compassion International

Compassion International exists as a Christian child advocacy ministry that releases children from spiritual, economic, social and physical poverty and enables them to become responsible, fulfilled Christian adults.

<http://www.compassion.com>

Conspire

Conspire wants every child and family to experience God's love and choose to follow Jesus for a lifetime. Conspire's mission is to provide resources, events and communities that envision, equip and encourage children's ministry leaders.

<http://www.willowcreek.com/children/index.asp>

OneHope

OneHope is a child evangelism organization dedicated to providing the word of God to children and youth of the world in whatever format will most relevant for their particular culture. OneHope has the word of God in easy to read formats for children which have been made culturally appropriate. They also have a video feature, GodMan, which tells the gospel message with trailers with cultural relevancy.

<http://www.onehope.org>

KidsQuest

KidsQuest USA is a 3-night event performed using the KidsQuest Kit and is an outreach ministry of the National Children's Ministries Agency in partnership with Assemblies of God churches across America. KidsQuest USA desires to partner with churches that can perform the crusade with home missions churches, military installation churches, Indian reservation ministries, Convoy of Hope outreaches, inner-city ministries and other ministries across our Fellowship who need an outreach event for kids.

<http://kidsquestusa.ag.org>

COMMUNITY DEVELOPMENT/ COMMUNITY HEALTH

ECHO

ECHO (Educational Concerns for Hunger Organization) is a non-profit, inter-denominational Christian organization located on a demonstration farm in North Fort Myers, Florida USA. ECHO has been assisting a global network of missionaries and development workers since 1981 and is currently serving agricultural workers in 180 countries. ECHO exists for one major reason, to help those working internationally with the poor be more effective, especially in the area of agriculture.

<http://www.echonet.org>

HealthCare Ministries

HealthCare Ministries is an international ministry of the Assemblies of God World Missions dedicated to global medical missions. In addition to medical teams, and general health education, offers training in Community Health Evangelism.

<http:///www.Healthcareministries.org>

LifeWind International

LifeWind is part of an international network of people who are passionately committed to holistic mission in the name of Jesus. They believe that practical action and prayer are equally indispensable for transforming lives physically, socially, and spiritually. Founded in 1980 and originally known as Medical Ambassadors International, they became a leading proponent of Community Health Evangelism (CHE), a proven strategy for bringing about profound changes in impoverished communities.

<http://www.lifewind.org>

Sustain Hope

Sustain Hope is an international ministry of the Assemblies of God World Missions that is focused on community development using appropriate technology. The team of missionaries is available to assist with participatory assessment, community dialogue and planning, market analysis and help with determining sustainable solutions. They prefer to work with and through local churches when possible.

<http://www.sustainhope.org>

World Vision

World Vision is a Christian relief, development and advocacy organization dedicated to working with children, families and communities to overcome poverty and injustice.

Inspired by Christian values, they are dedicated to working with the world's most vulnerable people. They serve all people regardless of religion, race, ethnicity or gender.

<http://www.wvi.org>

DISASTER RELIEF

American Red Cross

Since its founding in 1881 by visionary leader Clara Barton, the American Red Cross has been the nation's premier emergency response organization. As part of a worldwide movement that offers neutral humanitarian care to the victims of war, the American Red Cross distinguishes itself by also aiding victims of devastating natural disasters. Over the years, the organization has expanded its services, always with the aim of preventing and relieving suffering.

<http://www.redcross.org>

AmeriCares

AmeriCares is an international relief organization whose passion to help is matched by an ability to deliver. Whether it's an epic disaster or a daily struggle, AmeriCares goes to extraordinary lengths to ensure that medicines, medical supplies and aid reaches individuals in need wherever they are, whenever they need it.

<http://www.americares.org>

CARE

CARE is a leading humanitarian organization fighting global poverty. Women are at the center of CARE's community-based efforts to improve basic education, prevent the spread of HIV, increase access to clean water and sanitation, and expand economic opportunity and protect natural resources. CARE also delivers emergency aid to survivors of war and natural disasters, and helps people rebuild their lives. The organization has 38 national offices around the world.

<http://www.care.org>

Catholic Relief Services

Catholic Relief Services is the official international humanitarian agency of the Catholic community in the United States. The agency provides assistance to people in 99 countries and territories. CRS first provides direct assistance where needed, then encourages people to help with their own development and foster secure, productive, just communities that enable people to realize their potential. CRS responds to both natural disasters and complex emergencies, and approaches its emergency response programming through a framework of saving lives, supporting livelihoods and strengthening civil society.

<http://www.crs.org>

Convoy of Hope

Convoy of Hope mobilizes, resources, and trains churches and other groups to conduct community outreaches, respond to disasters, and direct other compassion initiatives in the United States and around the world.

<http://www.convoyofhope.org>

International Aid

Over the years, International Aid has responded to approximately 80 disasters around the world. With the help of our local partners and donors, we are able to support the rebuilding efforts for people in greatest need. Their emergency response goals are to support others in first response, replenish medical equipment and supplies, focus on rebuilding efforts to restore the area, and prevent disease with portable medical labs, water purification systems and hygiene kits.

<http://www.internationalaid.org/solutions/disaster-relief/>

Samaritan's Purse

Samaritan's Purse has done their utmost to follow Christ's command by going to the aid of the world's poor, sick, and suffering. They are an effective means of reaching hurting people in countries around the world with food, medicine, and other assistance in the name of Jesus Christ. This, in turn, earns them a hearing for the Gospel, the Good News of eternal life through Jesus Christ. Their emergency relief programs provide desperately needed assistance to victims of natural disaster, war, disease, and famine. As they offer food, water, and temporary shelter, they meet critical needs and give people a chance to rebuild their lives.

<http://www.samaritanspurse.org>

World Relief

In community with the local Church, World Relief envisions the most vulnerable people transformed economically, socially, and spiritually.

<http://community.wr.org>

ECONOMIC DEVELOPMENT

Opportunity International

This organization provides small business loans, savings, insurance and training in basic business practices to people living in chronic poverty.

<http://www.opportunity.org>

GOVERNMENTAL HELPS

World Health Organization

As the directing and coordinating authority on international health, the World Health Organization takes the lead within the UN system in the global health sector response to HIV/AIDS. The HIV/AIDS Department provides evidence-based, technical support to WHO member states to help them scale up treatment, care and prevention services, as well as drugs and diagnostic supply to ensure a comprehensive and sustainable response to HIV/AIDS.

    <http://www.who.int/hiv/en/>

HIV/AIDS

AIDS.gov

AIDS.gov serves as an information gateway to guide users to federal domestic HIV/AIDS information and resources. The goal is to give easy access to information on federal HIV/AIDS prevention, testing, treatment and research programs, policies and resources. AIDS.gov contains links to guide you to information on those topics.

    <http://www.aids.gov>

AIDSInfo

AIDSInfo is a service of the National Institutes of Health and the U.S. Department of Health and Human Services. The site offers the latest federally approved information on HIV/AIDS clinical research, treatment and prevention and medical practice guidelines for people living with HIV/AIDS, their families and friends, health care providers, scientists and researchers. It also includes clinical trials and medical guidelines.

<http://www.aidsinfo.nih.gov>

Cry Africa

Cry Africa is a ministry of Assemblies of God World Missions. Cry Africa was created in December 2002 as the continental HIV/AIDS initiative for sub-Saharan Africa.

<http://www.cryafrica.com>

Global AIDS Partnership

Global AIDS Partnership is an international ministry of the Assemblies of God World Missions which produces resources and offers training worldwide in HIV/AIDS awareness and intervention. Materials are available on the basic facts of HIV/AIDS, Testing and Counseling, Pastoral Care, Hospice Care, and Care of Children Infected or Affected with HIV. There is also a prayer guide for HIV and a bible study for youth. A small booklet about soccer and HIV is available for children.

<http://www.GlobalAIDSPartnership.org>

UNAIDS

UNAIDS, the Joint United Program on HIV/AIDS, brings together the efforts and resources of 10 UN system organizations to the global HIV/AIDS response. Cosponsors include UNHCR, UNICEF, WFP, UNDP, UNFPA, UNODC, ILO, UNESCO, WHO and the World Bank. It works in more than 75 countries worldwide. It has 5 focus areas including: leadership, tracking, monitoring and evaluation, civil society engagement and mobilization of resources.

Of special interest on this site are yearly updates on the global HIV/AIDS epidemic. UNAIDS harmonizes monitoring and evaluation approaches at global, regional and country levels to generate reliable and timely information on the epidemic and the response. Their statistics are considered highly reliable and are the most widely quoted around the globe. They also offer an enormous number of educational publications, dealing with every aspect of the epidemic.

<http://www.unaids.org>

World Vision

World Vision is a Christian humanitarian organization dedicated to working with children, families and their communities worldwide to reach their full potential by tackling the causes of poverty and injustice. Search "HIV" on this site to learn of their HIV/AIDS activities, and find current articles related to HIV/AIDS.

<http://www.WorldVision.org>

HUMAN TRAFFICKING

Administration for Children & Families, U. S. Department of Health & Human Services

The campaign to rescue and restore victims of human trafficking is described on this site and provides general information on human trafficking, including tools on how to identify people who may have been trafficked, and how to report suspected cases. Fact sheets are available in Spanish, Polish, Russian and Traditional Chinese.

<http://www.acf.hhs.gov/trafficking/index.html>

Amnesty International

AI's purpose is to protect people wherever justice, freedom, truth and dignity are denied. They investigate and expose abuses, educate and mobilize the public, and help transform societies to create a safer, more just world. AI has received the Nobel Peace Prize for their lifesaving work.

<http://www.amnestyusa.org/violence-against-women/end-human-trafficking/page.do?id=1108428>

Anti-Slavery International

Anti-Slavery International, founded in 1839, is the world's oldest international human rights organization and the only charity in the United Kingdom to work exclusively against slavery and related abuses. They work at local, national and international levels to eliminate the system of slavery around the world by urging governments of countries with slavery to develop and implement measures to end it; lobbying governments and intergovernmental agencies to make slavery a priority issue; supporting research to assess the scale of slavery in order to identify measures to end it; working with local organizations to raise public awareness of slavery; and educating the public about the realities of slavery and campaigning for its end.

<http://www.antislavery.org>

Coalition Against Trafficking in Women

The Coalition Against Trafficking in Women is creating, launching and supporting anti-trafficking projects in areas that few programs address: the links between prostitution and trafficking; challenging the demand for prostitution that promotes sex trafficking; and protecting the women and children who are its victims by working to curb legal acceptance and tolerance of the sex industry. Some articles are available in French and Spanish, and there are a few downloadable resources available.

<http://www.catwinternational.org>

Free the Slaves

Free the Slaves liberates slaves around the world, helps them rebuild their lives and researches real-world solutions to eradicate slavery forever. They use world-class research and compelling stories from the front lines of slavery to convince the powerful and the powerless that we can end slavery. Governments, the United Nations, businesses, communities, and each one of us has a role to play.

<http://www.freetheslaves.net>

Global Alliance Against Traffic in Women

The Global Alliance Against Traffic in Women is an alliance of more than 90 non-governmental organizations from all regions of the world. The GAATW International Secretariat is based in Bangkok, Thailand. It coordinates the activities of the Alliance, collects and disseminates information, and advocates on behalf of the Alliance at regional and international level. Member organizations include migrant rights organizations; anti-trafficking organizations; self-organized groups of migrant workers, domestic workers, survivors of trafficking and sex workers; human rights and women's rights organizations; and direct service providers.

<http://www.gaatw.org>

HumanTrafficking

The purpose of this web site is to bring government and NGOs together to cooperate and learn from each other's experiences in their efforts to combat human trafficking. The web site has country-specific information such as national laws, action plans and contact information on useful governmental agencies. It also has a description of NGO activities in different countries and their contact information. Many useful web site links are also provided.

<http://www.humantrafficking.org>

Human Trafficking Awareness Partnerships

The mission of the Human Trafficking Awareness Partnerships is to bring the issue of human trafficking to the forefront of public awareness by empowering individual communities to take action through education and the coordination of resources by creating partnerships of informed communities to share information, experiences and best practices in order to make the work of each partner more effective. The also work to extend efforts beyond local jurisdictions, and by supporting primary research and disseminating information.

<http://www.humantraffickingawareness.org>

Initiative Against Sexual Trafficking

The Initiative Against Sexual Trafficking is a distinctive partnership of organizations (spearheaded by The Salvation Army National Headquarters) united in their desire to abolish the sexual trafficking of women and children. IAST exists to create and equip a new abolition movement for the eradication of sexual trafficking, protection of survivors and prosecution of traffickers and exploiters.

<http://www.iast.net>

International Justice Mission

International Justice Mission is a human rights agency that secures justice for victims of slavery, sexual exploitation and other forms of violent oppression. IJM lawyers, investigators and aftercare professionals work with local officials to ensure immediate victim rescue and aftercare, to prosecute perpetrators and to promote functioning public justice systems.

<http://www.ijm.org>

Not For Sale Campaign

The Not For Sale Campaign equips and mobilizes activists to deploy innovative solutions to abolish slavery in their own backyards and across the globe. Facts and news items are presented. An excellent Bible study and college curriculum are available as free downloads.

<http://www.notforsalecampaign.org>

Polaris Project

This is the home page of Polaris Project, an organization involved in the fight against human trafficking. Named after the North Star that guided slaves towards freedom along the Underground Railroad, Polaris Project has been providing a comprehensive approach to combating human trafficking and modern-day slavery since 2002.

Polaris Project is one of the largest anti-trafficking organizations in the United States and Japan, with programs operating at international, national and local levels.

<http://www.polarisproject.org>

Project Rescue

Project Rescue is a ministry focused on trans-denominational aftercare of rescued women and girls. The rescue process begins when a victim is freed from the brothel and is considered complete only when she is emotionally, spiritually and physically healthy enough to begin a new life on her own. This holistic view of rescue includes providing a place of physical safety, medical care, counseling, literacy and vocational training, and spiritual development.

<http://www.projectrescue.com>

REFERENCES

Aaker, J., & Shumaker, J. (1994). *Looking back and looking forward: A participatory approach to evaluation.* Little Rock, AR: Heifer International.

Allen, R. (1962). *Missionary methods: St. Paul's or ours?* Grand Rapids, MI: Eerdmans.

Bueno, R. (2009). The Church and Community Transformation. Computer slide presentation given at Compassion Forum Seminar, St. Louis, MO, August 24, 2009.

Cannon, M. (2009). *Social Justice Handbook: Small steps for a better world.* Illinois: InterVarsity Press.

Chamber, R. (1997). *Whose reality counts: Putting the first last.* London: Intermediate Technology Publications.

Chester, T. (Ed). (2002). *Justice, mercy and humility: Integral mission and the poor.* Georgia: Paternoster Press.

Cheyne, J. (1996). *Incarnational agents: A guide to development ministry.* Alabama: New Hope.

Conrad, S. (2010). Moving from mercy to justice. Retrieved from <http://www.steveconrad.net/?p=35>

Corbett, S., & Fikkert, B. (2009). *When helping hurts: How to alleviate poverty without hurting the poor and yourself.* Chicago, IL: Moody Press.

Covey, S. (2004). *Seven habits of highly effective people.* New York: Free Press.

Darrow, K. & Saxenian, M. (1993). *Appropriate Technology Sourcebook: A Guide to Practical Books for Village and Small Community Technology.* Published by Appropriate Technology Institute.

Denison, N. (n. d.). 10 ways cell phones help people living in poverty. Retrieved from >http://dsc.discovery.com/technology/tech-10/cell-phones-help-nations.html>

Friedman, J. (1992). *Empowerment: The power of alternative development.* Cambridge, MA: Blackwell Publishers.

Gordon, G. (2003). *What if you got involved: Taking a stand against social injustice.* Georgia: Paternoster Press.

Grameen Bank. (2009).What is microcredit? Retrieved from <http://www.grameen-info.org/index.php?option=comcontent&task=view&id=28&Itemid=108>

Haugen, G. (1999). *Good news about injustice: A witness of courage in a hurting world.* Downers Grove/Leicester, IL: Intervarsity Press.

Hodges, M. (1953). *The indigenous church.* Springfield, MO: Gospel Publishing House.

Integral Mission (2001). Micah declaration on integral mission. Retrieved from <www.micahnetwork.org/en/integral-mission/micah-declaration>

Jayakaran, R. (1999). Holistic participatory learning and action: Seeing the spiritual and whose reality counts. In Myers, B. (Ed.), *Working with the poor: New insights and learnings from developmental practitioners*. Monrovia, CA: MARC.

Karnani, A. (2007) Downloaded on July 3, 2010. Retrieved from <http://www.ssireview.org/articles/entry/microfinance_misses_its_mark/>

Lupton, R. (2007). *Compassion, justice and the Christian life: Rethinking ministry to the poor*. Ventura, CA: Regal.

Miller, D., & Yamamori, T. (2007). *Global pentecostalism: The new face of Christian social engagement*. Berkley, CA: University of California Press.

Moyo, D. (2009). *Dead aid: Why aid is not working and how there is a better way for Africa*. New York: Farrar, Straus and Giroux.

Myers, B. L. (1999). *Walking with the poor: Principles and practices of transformational development*. New York, NY: Orbis Books.

Nouwen, H., McNeil, D., & Morrison, D. (1983). *Compassion: A reflection on the Christian life*. New York, NY: Doubleday.

Ott, G. (1993). Supporting national pastors—Let the buyer beware. *Evangelical Missions Quarterly*, July.

Relief Web. (2003). Sustainable relief in post-crisis situations: Transforming disasters into opportunities for sustainable development in human settlements. Retrieved from <http://www.reliefweb.int/rw/lib.nsf/db900SID/LHON-62DKLG?OpenDocument>

Salvato, R. (September, 2005). *Manual for training of disaster preparedness*. Manual presented at HealthCare

Ministries Seminar for Health Practitioner's Preparing to Respond to Disaster.

Sanford, D. (2008). Love: A paraphrase of 1 Corinthians 13. Retrieved from <http://kenyananalyst.wordpress.com/2008/02/12/love-a-paraphrase-of-1-corinthians-13/>

Satyavrata, I. (2009) Friends in mission: Following the wind and riding the wave, third lecture. Assemblies of God Theological Seminary Lectureship Series, November 2009.

Shaw, G. B. (n. d.). Retrieved from <http://thinkexist.com/quotation/the_only_man_who_behaves_sensibly_is_my_tailor-he/ 188548.html>

Solzhenitsyn, A. (n. d.). The nobel prize in literature. Retrieved from <http://nobelprize.org/nobel_prizes/literature/laureates/1970/solzhenitsyn-lecture.html>

Stearns, R. (2009). *The hole in our gospel: What does God expect of us? The answer changed my life and might just change the world.* Nashville, TN: Thomas Nelson Publishing.

Wheaton Consultation. (1983). The Consultation on the Church in Response to Human Need. Retrieved from <http://www.lausanne.org/all-documents/transformation-the-church-in-response-to-human-need.html>

World Health Organization. Disabilities. Retrieved from <http://www.who.int/topics/disabilities/en/>.

York, J. (2000). *Missions in the age of the spirit.* Springfield, MO: Logion Press.

INDEX